LA BELLE EPOQUE

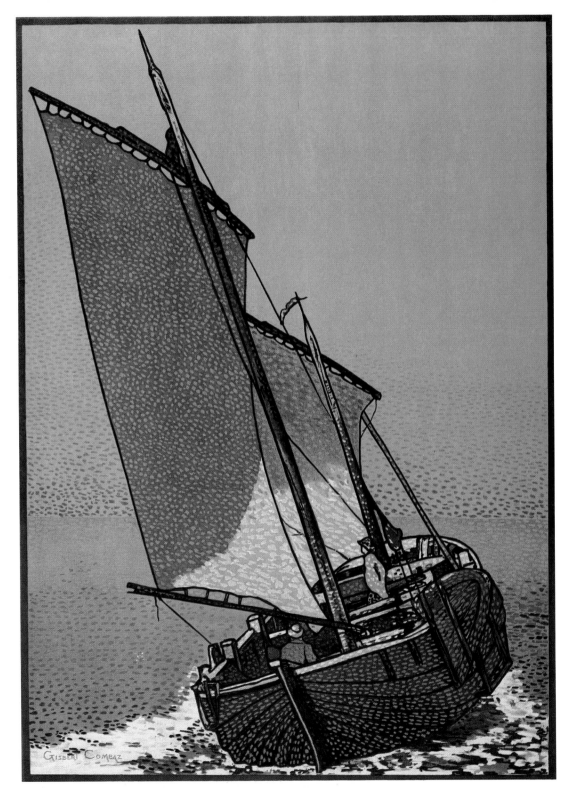

Catalogue No. 9.

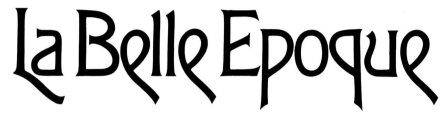

La Belle Epoque

MASTERWORKS BY COMBAZ, LÉO JO AND LIVEMONT

A Loan Exhibition from the Collection of L. Wittamer-De Camps

Introduction and Catalogue by
Yolande Oostens-Wittamer

Preface by Alan Fern

Essay by Hubert Durt

INTERNATIONAL EXHIBITIONS FOUNDATION
1980-1981

This catalogue is supported in part by grants from The Andrew W. Mellon Foundation
and Belgium Today, a program sponsored by the National Endowment for the Humanities
and the National Endowment for the Arts with the cooperation of the Government of Belgium.

Cover: Catalogue No. 31, *Wave,* by Combaz.

Contents

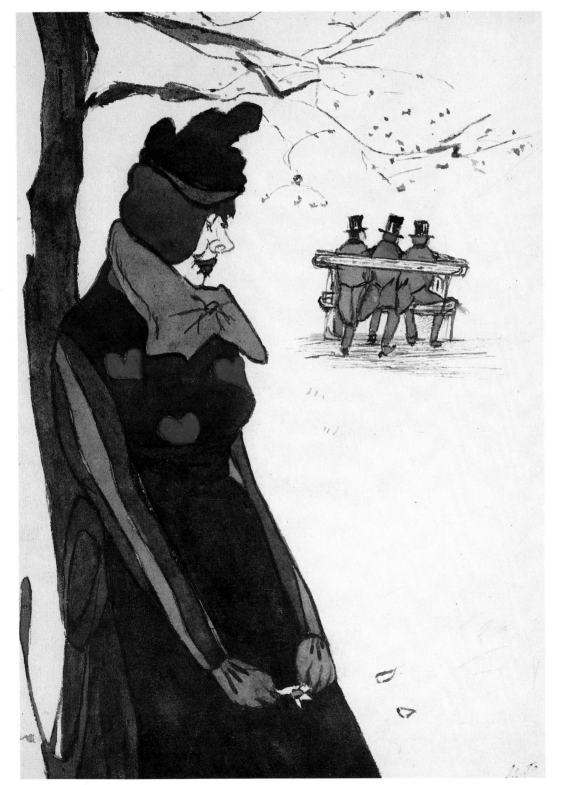

Catalogue No. 56.

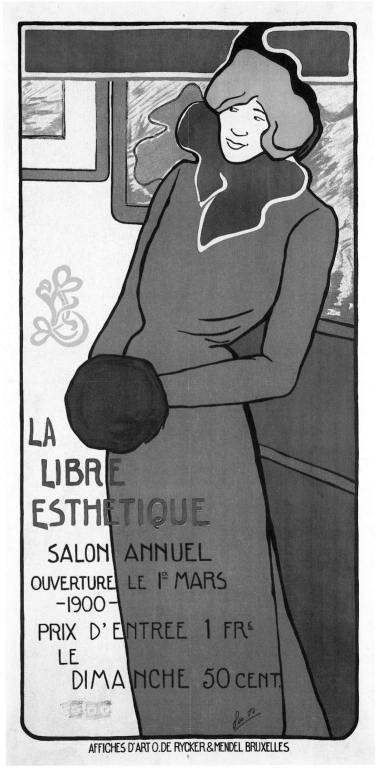

LA LIBRE ESTHETIQUE

SALON ANNUEL
OUVERTURE LE 1ᵉʳ MARS
—1900—
PRIX D'ENTREE 1 FRᶜ
LE
DIMANCHE 50 CENT.

AFFICHES D'ART O. DE RYCKER & MENDEL BRUXELLES

Catalogue No. 42.

Acknowledgments

It is with great pleasure that I write these few remarks as an introduction to the catalogue of "La Belle Epoque: Masterworks by Combaz, Léo Jo and Livemont." This is the second exhibition of Belgian posters, watercolors and drawings from the Wittamer-De Camps collection that the International Exhibitions Foundation has been privileged to organize, and we have thoroughly enjoyed the opportunity to renew our association.

We are deeply indebted to M. and Mme Louis Wittamer-De Camps and family for this generous loan from their splendid collection, housed in their charming residence at the Hôtel Solvay in Brussels. The catalogue, which details with such enthusiasm the history of the three artists and their works, has been written by the Wittamer's daughter, Yolande Oostens-Wittamer, and we are grateful not only for her scholarly contribution to the catalogue but also for the help that she and her parents have rendered throughout the organization of the tour.

We also wish to express our gratitude to Alan Fern, Director for Special Collections at the Library of Congress, who has written the catalogue preface and has responded thoughtfully to our many queries at every stage of the project. Warm thanks go also to our good friend Margaret Breitenbach for her excellent translation of the catalogue introduction; to Judy Raak for her assistance in translating the entries; and to Taffy Swandby for editing the manuscript and seeing the catalogue through the press.

The publication has been beautifully printed by The Arts Publisher, Inc. with the capable assistance of James Witt of that firm and graphic designer Raymond Geary. It is supported in part by grants from The Andrew W. Mellon Foundation and from Belgium Today, a program sponsored by the National Endowment for the Humanities and the National Endowment for the Arts with the cooperation of the Government of Belgium.

The directors of the museums participating in the tour have been cooperative at every stage, and in particular we wish to thank Director James Brown and his staff at The Society of the Four Arts in Palm Beach. Finally, I wish to express my gratitude to the staff of the Foundation, notably Christina Flocken, for attending to the many complex practical details involved in the organization of the tour.

ANNEMARIE H. POPE
President
International Exhibitions Foundation

May this exhibition revive, and permit us to share, the joy and audacity so tenderly inscribed by these artists in their work.

I wish to thank all those who have assisted in its preparation, in particular the following: Annemarie H. Pope, President of the International Exhibitions Foundation, and her staff; Alan Fern, Director for Special Collections, Library of Congress; Hubert Durt, Membre de l'École Française d'Extrême-Orient and Editor of *Hōbōgirin;* Jacqueline Gesquière, professor of literature and philosophy; Arthur Grosemans, painter and lithographer emeritus; Louis Loose, former head of the Photographic Service at l'Institut Royal du Patrimoine Artistique; the late photographer, Morian; Bernadette Laloux, professor of drawing; the families of the artists, especially Mme Suzanne Combaz and Mme Edith Van Overstraeten; and Juliette Boutans, secretary.

YOLANDE OOSTENS-WITTAMER

Preface

The works in this exhibition celebrate an artistic movement, a nation, and a collection.

The movement is Art Nouveau, the remarkable international style that seemed to burst forth in every part of the world in the last decade of the 19th century. The ideal of Art Nouveau was to create a universe in which both practical and artistic objects shared a sensuous use of materials and colors. Art works and manufactured objects utilized a vocabulary of characteristic lines and forms, and even a lamp or table might be adorned with images making symbolic reference to moods, to emotions, and to the beauties of the natural world. Moreover, the previously utilitarian poster was elevated to a higher status by Art Nouveau designers, and became one of the most characteristic and ubiquitous heralds of the new style.

The nation is Belgium, a center of artistic activity, education, and exhibitions in the 1890s. The painters, architects, and designers in this tiny nation had an exceptional impact. The publishers of art journals and posters were energetic and imaginative, so their products were transmitted everywhere to satisfy the curiosity about the latest aesthetic trends. Artists and designers from France, England, Germany, Austria, and the United States came to Belgium to display their work, while Belgians like Rops, Horta, and Van de Velde often went abroad, to teach, learn and work. Like the playwright Maeterlinck and the composer César Franck, these artists attained international stature not enjoyed since the 17th century by natives of Brussels, Antwerp, Bruges, and Ghent. As this exhibition demonstrates, poster artists were central to this international cultural outpouring.

The works shown here come from a single Belgian collection, that of M. and Mme L. Wittamer-De Camps. From the moment they bought a superb town house by the architect Horta—the famous Hôtel Solvay, in Brussels—the Wittamer family dedicated themselves to collecting posters, prints, decorative arts, paintings, and books by the Belgian artists of the 1890s. With discrimination, ingenuity and energy they have assembled their collection, studied it, and shared it in a series of exhibitions with audiences around the world. In particular, their holdings seem an endless resource for the exploration of the graphic arts. Once again we are indebted to M. and Mme Wittamer, and their daughter, Yolande Oostens-Wittamer, for sharing with us the delightful posters they possess. In their time these posters carried the reputation of Belgium abroad as they proclaimed the virtues of Belgian products, places, technology, music, and literature. Today, they travel again, connecting us through time and space with a nation, a period, and a culture of extraordinary vitality.

ALAN FERN

Introduction

This exhibition brings together one hundred works by three Belgian artists of the Art Nouveau period: Gisbert Combaz, Léo Jo (Léontine Joris) and Privat Livemont. It is the sequel to the original exhibition organized in 1970-71 by the International Exhibitions Foundation, and dedicated to the emergence of poster art in Belgium.[1]

With the exception of certain posters, the majority of the items displayed here come directly from the studios of the artists; they have remained unknown even to connoisseurs since the beginning of the century. Once again, we are delighted to share with the American public the discovery of works which have contributed to an awareness of a distinctly Belgian art form, particularly in the fields of decorative and commercial art.

Furthermore, the fact that these three artists have themselves very distinct personalities gives us the advantage of seeing complementary points of view of this exceptionally fertile period.

Gisbert Combaz, who was thirty-one years old in 1900, was trained as a lawyer. Art, however, was his true vocation, at three levels: as an artist, as an art historian (he was an Orientalist) and as a teacher. An article by Hubert Durt (see p. 36) treats the subject of Combaz as Orientalist. As an artist "who devotes himself with intelligence and initiative to all branches of commercial art,"[2] Combaz was to be found among the leaders in the international art salons, such as *La Libre Esthétique* (see Cat. nos. 2-9) and was kept busy with projects, such as that for the *Maison d'Art* (Cat. No.11.) An outstanding professor, he taught for over forty-five years.

Léo Jo, slightly younger than Combaz, was a doctor's daughter. Self-taught, she identified herself with the spirit of her contemporaries, and playfully unmasked them with mischievous caricatures. *Vita brevis, ridentes eamus.* With her respect for life and for a sense of proportion, she discovered in laughter her source of strength, and in graphic art her true vocation. Her humorous sketches were acclaimed, and published in several Belgian and foreign periodicals.

Privat Livemont, ten years older than Léo Jo, divided his life between his teaching at the Académie of Schaerbeek and his thriving business enterprises. On his letterhead was inscribed: "Art posters and prints. Decorations for apartments. Traditional and modern styles. Sgraffiti." His Sunday lectures drew a full audience. A talented lithographer, his reputation spread throughout Europe and well beyond.

The delicacy of his female figures reflects a deep sensitivity, but an underlying seriousness in some sketches reveals another, no less valid, aspect of his concern.

One important question arises: How did the artists and the public view the subject matter? Where was the challenge, the intense satisfaction, the inner stimulation. Here it is not a question of the technique, but of the depth of the creative process itself.

It is true that a work of art is born anew in the eyes of an admirer, but it is also fascinating to try to see it through the eyes of the artist himself. The artist reveals his feelings, and his period, through a thousand sometimes scarcely perceptible clues. These clues help us to better utilize outside information and to connect the forces at work in any given period through the artist's own experiences of life. That is why the historical references added to the technical descriptions in the catalogue are as varied as possible: a musical score, a strophe from a poem, a description of the public's infatuation with orchids and their cultivation, a discussion of the changing trend in lingerie design—all serve to enhance our understanding of the total environment in which Combaz, Léo Jo and Livemont were producing the works exhibited here.

One thing is certain. The new awareness that Belgium experienced at the end of the last century created an astonishing burst of activity throughout the country in all fields of endeavor. Artists, closely linked to changes in society, to some extent shaped a new vision of art:

"There are some fortunate periods in which a young shoot is suddenly grafted onto an old tree. At such a time there are places in which opposing currents meet and swirl against each other, with an antagonistic force that time will later dissipate; for a common aspiration, more or less precise, will strengthen them while opposing them, and sometimes ideas coincide and serve as a mutual stimulus before they split off, evolve, and go their separate ways. In the 1880s Brussels was just such a place."[3]

Let us look briefly at two corollary movements. First, we should emphasize the enthusiastic interest shown in the decorative arts by some of the greatest artists, which then provided a rallying point for those whose credo was *L'Art dans Tout* (Art in Everything); *L'Art pour Tous* (Art for Everyone) and *L'Art pour l'Art* (Art for Art's Sake).

This explosion of *Art Nouveau* was quite naturally bound to lead to a reevaluation of art education. Later we shall touch briefly on the reforms introduced by the architect, Victor Horta, at the Académie des Beaux-Arts in Brussels. This occurred in 1912, at a time when Gisbert Combaz was on the faculty.

DECORATIVE AND COMMERCIAL ART

"In the areas of decorative and commercial art, Belgium has for many years attracted attention to an artistic activity whose influence and repercussions have been felt throughout Europe. Though in the past she was content with sterile imitations, around 1885 there was a sudden awakening—a renaissance— which by its charming spontaneity and novelty kindled the sparks of enthusiasm among its artists, vastly encouraged their initiative, and brought about trends of opinion that completely reversed the contemporary esthetic."[4]

Octave Maus, who wrote the above, was a lawyer, a musician, the secretary of the *Groupe des XX*, and the founder and director of the annual international salons sponsored by *La Libre Esthétique*. He was directly involved with *Trente Années de Lutte pour l'Art* (Thirty Years of Struggle for Art), the period to which he here alludes and which was the subject of a book by that title, written by his wife, Madeleine.[5] He explains the depth of this "revolution that was both moral and artistic" which was initiated in England in 1861 by William Morris, Ford Madox Brown, Philip Webb and Edward Burne-Jones, co-founders of the famous shop at Red Lion Square.[6]

"By its new conception of art this reform covered more than modifications of line, color and form. It required of ordinary people a response that for a long time had been expected only of the élite. It involved the people in esthetic pleasures by introducing into their lives the scent of a new ideal. It equated art with the notion of work, expressing the hope, as William Morris put it, that art should give as much pleasure to the maker as to the user."[7]

"But if it is right to give credit to the poet of Hammersmith for having reconciled the cult of Beauty with the demands of everyday life, it would be wrong not to recognize the initiative of the Belgian artists, who subscribed to his theories, and to think of them as only his disciples and imitators. What radically distinguishes them from their illustrious predecessors is that they took off at the precise point at which the former had stopped. Instead of being inspired by the past, they dared to look to the future."[8]

The Belgians took up the torch from the English, who had allowed themselves to be outdistanced, and fenced in by beautiful formulas, and whose work was repetitious and redolent of archaic memories. They freed themselves resolutely from the past, and the French, Germans and Dutch followed suit. It is significant that the first copy of *L'Art Décoratif* that came out in Paris in October 1898 (and appeared simultaneously in Munich) was devoted entirely to Henri Van de Velde.

The public was sometimes deeply hostile towards new ideas, but once under way, the impulse towards change was profound and vital.

Commercial art acquired social status when architects of the caliber of Victor Horta integrated each element of furnishing and decoration into an architecture that was sound, robust and new, representative of the needs and tastes of the owner (such as the large private houses, Hôtel Tassel and Hôtel Solvay, built in 1892 and 1894 respectively).

Private groups were launched: the *Maison d'Art* 1894-1900 in Brussels (Cat. No. 11); *Onze Kunst* in Courtrai; *Scalden* in Antwerp. These groups furthered the work of the salons of the *Cercle des XX*; of *La Libre Esthétique*; of the circle *Pour l'Art* and of the *Société des Beaux-Arts*, bringing artists and businessmen together, circulating new ideas and serving as permanent sales outlets.

After an intense struggle, an official hurdle was cleared on the occasion of the Brussels Exposition of 1897. The Belgian government granted to commercial art the same rights (free exhibition space and transportation) accorded to works of art, or so-called works of art.

> "The efforts made by the Organizing Committee to arrive at a permanent solution of this important question of principle will be particularly appreciated in France and in England, where the bureaucracy has thwarted negotiations leading to the same goal."[9]

French and English artists, not being allowed to exhibit commercial or decorative art objects in the Beaux-Arts section, preferred to withdraw rather than to find themselves among the manufacturers and merchants.

More than sixty Belgian artists responded to the appeal of the previously mentioned committee. Among them were Combaz and Livemont, as well as Knopff, Lemmen, Van Rysselberghe, Finch, Hankar, Crespin, Van der Stappen, Meunier, Toussaint and Mignot.

However, in spite of the great impetus given in this direction, they still suffered from official rebuffs, and from the timid reactions of big business (with the exception of Val Saint Lambert). Belgian artists, who had been acclaimed at the International Exhibition of Decorative Art held in Turin in 1902, found themselves denied admission to the gallery of the Beaux-Arts at the International Exhibition in Brussels and to the Palais des Beaux-Arts at the World Exhibition held in Liège in 1905.

Maus reported sadly that "the small collection of modern art objects acquired by the government had waited for fifteen years to be installed at the Musée des Arts Décoratifs."[10]

> "Imagine the surprise of a German, a Dutchman or an Austrian who comes to Belgium to study the origins and development of the art to which Belgium has given birth, and finds no trace of it, either in our museums or in our exhibitions!"[11]

Thus, little by little, Belgium allowed itself to lose the advantage of the headstart it had enjoyed. Maus concludes his report with a ringing appeal:

> "The artists are tireless in their initiative. As we have said, the skills they have demonstrated in all branches of applied art have been universally recognized. Let us support them. Let us introduce a theoretical and technical course of instruction that will address today's needs. Let us interest both industry and the public in what they are doing . . . and finally, let there be both permanent and temporary exhibition space reserved for them in the museums."[12]

REFORM OF ART INSTRUCTION

A reform of the system of art education was patently becoming more and more urgent. Just as traditional art was burdened with pastiches, instruction was hampered by artificial rules. Courses in painting and sculpture were freed from arbitrary canons in favor of an increased observation of nature. However, courses in architecture remained inadequate. Attempts at reform were made on several occasions, either by the professors as individuals or more officially, by the authorities. Combaz and Livemont were both professors whose words carried weight, because of their success in teaching the modern principles in which they themselves believed, and which they applied with sensitivity. Around 1912, Mabille, the Director-General for Fine Arts, wishing to thoroughly upgrade the instruction at the Académie des Beaux-Arts, had reports prepared by several experts. Above all, he sought the advice of the architect, Victor Horta. The latter obliged by sending him a complete program of revision, stating bluntly:

> "In my career I have suffered for a long time from the gaps in the education that I received. I have seen plenty of my colleagues who were no better prepared than I was, and every day I am aware of the insufficient knowledge of the young architects with whom we are expected to collaborate in our work."[13]

Mabille did not hesitate. He nominated Horta to be a professor at the Académie, and then made him its director so that he could implement his program, which was designed to give each student a thorough, personal training consistent with his abilities, his tastes, and the increasing complexity of the problems to be solved. Horta's program was divided into three progressive stages, each of which culminated in its own diploma: 1) *the school of drawing*—a three-year, non-specialized program open to all students age twelve or older, which emphasized mastery of "the correct use of the pencil . . . a tool complete in itself"[14] through courses in Drawing from Nature, Human Anatomy, and the like; 2) *the technical school*, whose four-year curriculum was designed to produce "an elite class of workmen, having an in-depth, theoretical knowledge of their métier,"[15] and 3) *the advanced course,* in which graduates of the preceding two programs would receive three years' specialized training "geared to the production of architects, engravers, painters and sculptors."[16]

In short, Horta wanted to revolutionize (in his words, "dynamite") the system of art education:

> "And through the yawning gap the passers-by will be able to enter! And I will shatter the windows, too, so that the sound of lessons can mingle with the murmur of Nature; so that the outside air may mix with the air inside, so that there might be, finally, only a single common atmosphere, for the regeneration of the blood of mankind."[17]

YOLANDE OOSTENS-WITTAMER

NOTES

1. Y. Oostens-Wittamer, *La Belle Epoque: Belgian Posters, Watercolors and Drawings* from the collection of L. Wittamer-De Camps, Washington, D.C., 1970.
2. Octave Maus, "L'Art appliqué en Belgique," in *L'Art et la Vie en Belgique, 1830-1905,* Brussels, 1921, p. 123.
3. F.-C. Legrand, *Le Groupe des XX et son Temps,* Musées Royaux des Beaux-Arts, Brussels, Feb. 17-Apr. 8, 1962, p. 17; Georges H. Dumont, *La Vie Quotidienne en Belgique sous la Règne de Léopold II (1865-1909),* Librairie Hachette, Paris, 1974.
4. O. Maus, *op. cit.,* p. 117.
5. Madeleine O. Maus in her book *Trente Années de Lutte pour l'Art* (Brussels, 1926) gives a precise but poetic description of the birth and subsequent growth of these artistic movements—"the chronicle of a period of struggle," in her own words.
6. O. Maus, *op. cit.,* p. 117.
7. Octave Maus had great respect for the common man, and he replied as follows to a letter from a reader of *L'Art Moderne:* "The day will come when in Belgium and elsewhere the people will have obtained the rights they have demanded. There is no doubt that we shall then see the flower of an imperishable art, reborn from a popular source, and shining in the light of a new dawn" (from "L'Art et le Peuple," in *L'Art Moderne,* Brussels, September 22, 1901, pp. 315-317).
8. O. Maus, "L'Art appliqué en Belgique," pp. 117, 118.
9. Anonymous, "Les Industries d'art à l'Exposition de Bruxelles," in *L'Art Moderne,* April 18, 1897, p. 126.
10. O. Maus, *op. cit.,* p. 124.
11. *Ibid.,* p. 125.
12. *Ibid.,* pp. 125, 126.
13. Victor Horta, *Projet de réorganisation des cours de l'Académie Royale des Beaux-Arts de Bruxelles et de l'École des Arts Décoratifs. Plans d'études et programmes des cours,* Brussels, 1912, p. 3.
14. Victor Horta, *Discours,* speech given on November 23, 1913 at a prize-giving ceremony at the Académie Royale des Beaux-Arts and École des Arts Décoratifs de Bruxelles, Brussels, 1914, p. 15.
15. Victor Horta, *Discours,* pp. 15-16.
16. *Ibid.,* pp. 16, 17.
17. *Ibid.,* p. 11.

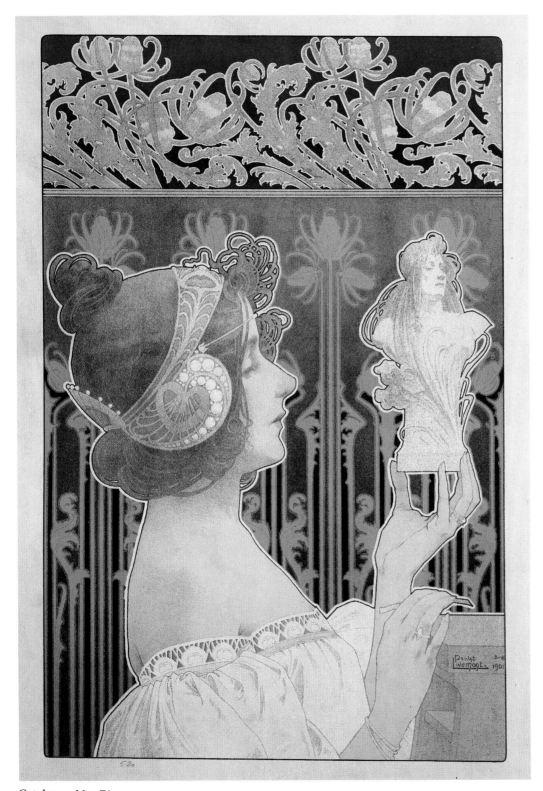

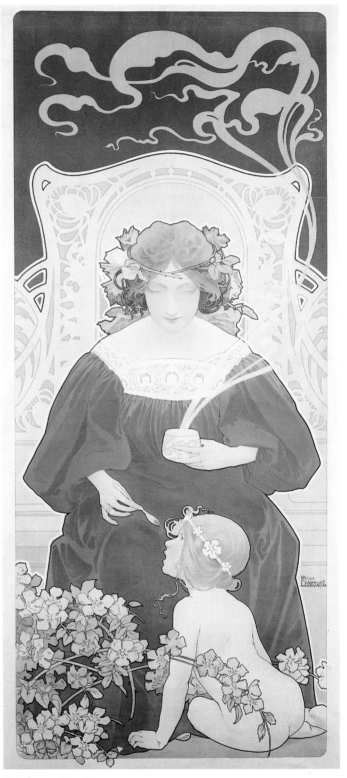

Catalogue No. 71.

Catalogue No. 96.

Catalogue

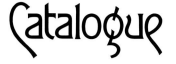

NOTE ON THE CATALOGUE

The entries are divided into three parts:
1. Title and date of work; technique in which the work was executed; dimensions in centimeters (height preceding width); all identifying marks (such as the artist's signature, printer's name, inscriptions, and text of the advertisement if the work is not illustrated); L. Wittamer-De Camps Collection accession number; publications in which the work itself or some form of the work has been reproduced, when such information provides the reader with additional relevant data.
2. The explanatory text.
3. Summary bibliography, when appropriate.

LITERATURE CITED IN ABBREVIATED FORM

A.B.   : A. Demeure de Beaumont, *L'Affiche belge* (Toulouse, 1897).

A & D   : *Art et Décoration*, a monthly illustrated periodical of modern art (Paris, 1897-present).

A.E.I.   : M. Bauwens, *Les Affiches Etrangères Illustrèes* (Paris, 1897); pp. 89-139 deal with Belgium.

E & A   : *L'Estampe et l'Affiche*, bulletin of the society of the same name, organ of the society of artists, printers, and amateurs of prints and posters (Paris, 1897-1899).

Maus   : M.O. Maus, *Trente années de lutte pour l'art* (Brussels, 1926).

St. P   Universal Exhibition of St. Petersburg: catalogue of international exhibition of illustrated posters, vol. 1, pt. 2, Belgian section, pp. 12-19 (St. Petersburg, 1897).

The P   : *The Poster*, a monthly illustrated periodical published under the direction of Hugh Macleay (London, 1898-1900).

GISBERT CORNEILLE HENRI PAUL COMBAZ
(Antwerp 1869–Schaerbeek 1941)

Professor of drawing at the State Institute of Agronomy in Gembloux (1895-1900), Professor of Decorative Art at the School of Decorative and Industrial Art at Ixelles (1898-1940), Professor of Art History at the New University (later the Institute of Advanced Studies of Belgium) in 1905, of which he will also be a member of the Managing Committee, and Professor of Ornamental Composition at the Royal Academy of Fine Arts and the School of Decorative Arts of Brussels (1912), and founder-president of the Belgian Society of Oriental Studies (1934), Combaz was also an Oriental scholar as well as a lawyer, painter and artist.

His father, Paul Combaz, a major in the Belgian Army and an archaeologist, had him study law; after practicing law for one year, Gisbert abandoned the bar in order to devote himself to art and take courses at the Royal Academy of Brussels.

Fascinated by Asia, he became a well-reputed Oriental scholar of whom Hubert Durt speaks warmly and knowledgeably in his essay "Gisbert Combaz, Artist and Orientalist" (see p. 36).

Combaz' work environment reflected his tastes. He surrounded himself with marvelous red and gold Chinese lacquer-ware furniture. "His collection, which he was happy to show, . . . contained several very rare pieces, such as the heads from the Lung-Men caves, the first to be seen in [Belgium]. But Combaz also collected all sorts of ceramics, particularly animal figures, both Chinese and Japanese, and potteries from all those countries which, following the example of the Japanese, sought inspiration in folk pottery. One can say that in this regard Combaz was a forerunner of this efflorescence of pottery craft which we are experiencing today. Combaz himself was very closely involved in the first [Belgian] attempts in this genre." (Lavachery, col. 171).

Combaz the artist was considered "a devoted friend and a man of taste" (Maus, p. 165). He was involved with *La Libre Esthétique* from 1897 on and exhibited there in 1897, 1898, 1899, 1901, 1903, 1908, 1912, and 1914, often designing the poster for the exhibition. He engaged in research in the decorative arts, giving life to ordinary, everyday objects by using diverse representations. Water and fire, wind, flowers, animals from the earth and sea, irridescent insects filled his youthful dreams which, as an artist, he shared with his contemporaries. His art was close to the worlds of the Belgian and the Oriental poets, intermingling recollections of both, and transcending time and space with its powerful inspiration.

He passed all this along to his students, since he had "a strong feeling for teaching . . . [and] . . . knew how to awaken [in them] the taste for research and a feeling for unusual beauty" (Lavachery, cols. 171, 172). His strength was in knowing how to respect his students' intuitions: when he corrected a drawing, he would never draw directly on the paper but would instead indicate with his hand a more generous line, a more dynamic setting. The student would see the new possibilities but at the same time would retain his choice of expression.

Certain characteristics of the artist's work merit our attention. Combaz creates forms surrounded by a nervous, supple, vibrant arabesque—for example, thistle leaves and the spaces between them (Cat. No. 4), mountain peaks (Cat. No. 5), the hems of lawyers' robes (Cat. No. 1); his monogram is treated in the same manner. He did not exclude the use of stippling or of looser forms, but the above characteristics were inherent to his nature and to his hand.

After the forms were established, Combaz laid on colors in refined, flat tints, often very luminous. Sometimes he freed himself from these flat areas of color and worked the tones in relief, or in spots and points, but the form, although veiled, remained the guide. For *La Libre Esthétique* of 1906 and on several other occasions, Combaz utilized a neo-impressionist technique in the poster.

His compositions are always centered without confusion on a principal subject (such as a peacock, eagle, or person), even if sometimes a tangle of details makes it more complex. The text, in elegant calligraphy, is often set under the picture. These detailed posters retain a surprising freshness, harmoniously mixing in diverse ways the Orient, dreams and reality.

A.E.I., pp. 103, 104, 111-113, 124; J. Capart and Dr. A. Spruyt, "Gisbert Combaz," *Bulletin des Musées Royaux d'Art et d'Histoire*, Brussels, 3rd series, 13th year, no. 1, Jan-Feb. 1941, p. 2; communications from Mme Suzanne Combaz, the artist's daughter; A.B. pp. 61-62; R. Grousset and J. Auboyer, "Gisbert Combaz," excerpt from *Mélanges Chinois et Bouddhiques*, Bruges, vol. 8; Henri Lavachery, "Combaz, Gisbert," in *Biographie Nationale*, Royal Academy of Belgium, Brussels, 1965, vol. 33, pt. 1, cols. 169-173; Maus, pp. 165, 172, 215, 220, 227, 233, 255, 285, 293, 297, 361, 381, 435 and 463; Octave Maus, "Les industries d'art au Salon de La Libre Esthétique," A&D, Paris, 1897, vol. 1, p. 48; 1898, vol. 1, pp. 97-100, 102; 1899, vol. 1, pp. 100-101; M. Rassenfosse, "Le peintre G. Combaz," in *L'Expansion belge*, 2nd year, no. 6, June 1929, pp. 25-28.

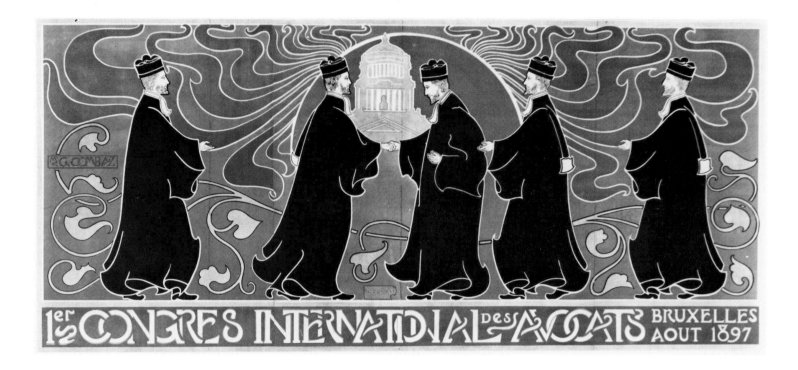

1. PREMIER CONGRÈS INTERNATIONAL DES AVOCATS. 1897

Lithograph in light green, dark green, red and black. Eight stones were required to print this poster, since there were two sheets of paper and each was printed with all four colors.

78.0 × 159.3 cm.

Me (i.e., "Maître") G. Combaz (on this occasion the artist indicated in his signature that he was a lawyer, or "Maître"); J. L. Goffart, Bruxelles. Coll. W.D. No. 42.

The lawyers come to life on a background of red and green, the colors of the City of Brussels. The site of the meeting is indicated by the profile of the dome of the Brussels Palace of Justice, built between 1866 and 1883 by the architect Poelaert.

Twenty-two countries, including the United States, Russia and Japan, responded to a questionnaire prepared by the Congress, which was presided over by Edmond Picard (1836-1924), lawyer, jurist, man of letters, and connoisseur of the arts. In 1881 Picard founded the *Journal des Tribunaux* and, with his friend and colleague Octave Maus, the magazine *l'Art Moderne;* in 1894 he opened the *Maison d'Art* in Brussels, on the Avenue of the Golden Fleece (avenue de la Toison d'Or).

(See Combaz: *A la Toison d'Or*, No. 11; Privat Livemont: *Ville de Bruxelles*, No. 94)

Journal des Tribunaux, Brussels, 1897, col. 897-944, 1177-1204, 1281-1304, 1306; Fédération des Avocats Belges, *Omnia Fraterne, 1886-1911*, Brussels, 1912, pp. 24-26; Michèle Coraine and Phil Mertens, under the auspices of the international association of art critics, with the assistance of Unesco, *Archives de l'art contemporain*, international Bulletin no. 2, 1965, Belgian section, p. 4.

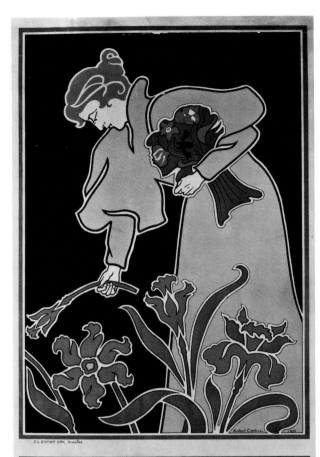

2. LA LIBRE ESTHÉTIQUE (GATHERING FLOWERS). 1897

Lithograph in yellow, red, light green and blue.

71.5 × 40.8 cm.

Gisbert Combaz 1897; J. L. Goffart, lith. Bruxelles. Coll. W.D. No. 39.

". . .on lie une pensée ardente aux moindres choses:
à l'éveil d'un bourgeon, au déclin d'une rose. . ."

Emile Verhaeren, "Les heures d'après-midi," 1905

Three "cathedrals" by Monet, six Gauguins from Tahiti, and a brilliant ensemble of works by Albert Besnard charmed the visitors to the Salon of 1897. The graphic arts were represented by *L'Estampe originale* and the beautiful collection of the *Peintres graveurs*. There were also large numbers of art books, metal objects from the Birmingham School of Handicrafts, first exhibits by Combaz, dining room furniture made in wood from the Congo by the architect Victor Horta, and architectural elements by Plumet and Voysey. Verhaeren spoke at a meeting held in support of the Verlaine monument to be erected in the Luxembourg Gardens; Vincent d'Indy and Isaac Albeniz performed pieces by Destouches and Rameau on the harpsichord.

Maus, pp. 215-225.

3. LA LIBRE ESTHÉTIQUE (PEACOCK). 1898

Lithograph in yellow, blue, dark blue, red, dark bistre, special green.

72.7 × 43.5 cm.

Gisbert Combaz 1898; chromolith. J.L. Goffart, Bruxelles. Their mark appended to the fiscal stamp is dated 18 February 1898. Coll. W.D. No. 51 bis.

The *Heure embrasée* (Hour of Illumination) acquired by the Weimar Museum, some preparatory studies, some landscapes and portraits, including one of P. Signac, formed a consignment of works by Van Rysselberghe that was greatly admired at the 1898 Salon. Ensor showed, as always. George Minne participated with some of his works—the *Trois saintes femmes* and *L'Homme agenouillé*—along with Maillol and a series of German artists (including Liebermann) invited through Van de Velde. The Dutchman Thorn Prikker, taking up a Javanese process, exhibited some batiks on silk, thereby showing the public a new style. There were a large number of porcelains from Copenhagen, carpets from Brangwyn, and some works by L. Tiffany.

The Impressionist masters had to refuse their invitations to *La Libre Esthétique* because of their contracts with their dealers, according to a letter of Sisley.

Maus, pp. 227-231.

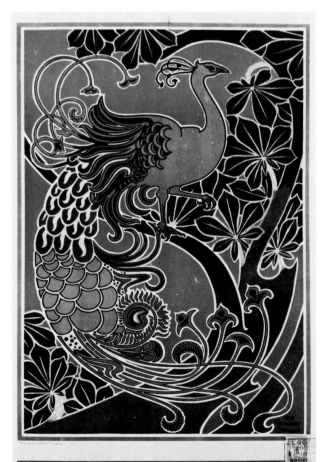

4. LA LIBRE ESTHÉTIQUE (TREE AND SUN). 1899

Lithograph in yellow, flesh, light blue, dark blue, dark green and red.

74.0 × 44.0 cm.

Gisbert Combaz 1899; chromolith. J.L. Goffart, Bruxelles. The text, at bottom, reads: La Libre Esthétique Salon Annuel: Musée Moderne: de 10 à 5 H[eure]s, Ouverture: 23 février, Prix d'entrée: 1 fr., le dimanche: 50 c.
Coll. W.D. No. 43.

Felicien Rops died in August, 1898; the following spring *La Libre Esthétique* exhibited in his honor an important selection of his works. Rassenfosse presented the illustrations of Baudelaire's *Fleurs du Mal;* Finch sent a very beautiful set of pottery from Finland; the Vereinigte Werkstätte (United Workshop) of Munich participated. Rodin obstinately refused to loan his *Balzac,* which had been unfavorably received by public officials in Paris, for fear that the work would again be misunderstood.

From the point of view of graphics, the composition of the tree in this poster recalls the work of the painter Tseng Hou Hsi, *The poet Li Pai drinking in moonlight,* which is reproduced in *La poésie chinoise,* an anthology edited by Patricia Guillermaz (Poitiers, 1960, p. 144).

Maus, pp. 233-240.

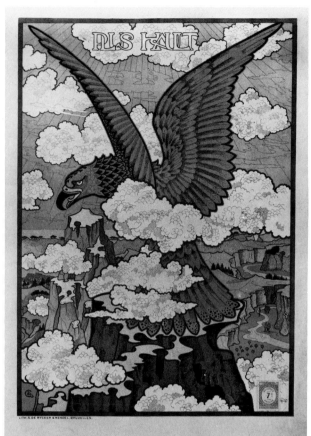

5. LA LIBRE ESTHÉTIQUE (PLUS HAUT). 1900

Lithograph in yellow, orange, mauve, light blue and dark blue.

74.3 × 43.2 cm.

G.C.; lith. O. De Rycker & Mendel, Bruxelles.
Coll. W.D. No. 45.

> *"J'ai traversé tout ce qu'ont traversé toutes les rivières,*
> *tous les détroits du globe,*
> *J'ai pris pour tremplin les péninsules et les hauts rocs*
> *inébranlables*
> *pour crier de là-haut: salut au monde!*
>
> Emile Verhaeren

The Salon of 1900 was distinguished by the works of Evenepoel, who had died 27 December 1899. Attention also centered on important works by

Zuloaga showing a disturbing and harsh Spain, on pastels by Roussel, plaster casts by Bourdelle, a wonderful contribution by Signac, the *Coq* by Ensor, and *l'Amour des âmes* by Delville.

A lecture by Thomas Braun paved the way for one by Francis Jammes: "Poets Against Literature." Gide, who attended the lecture with an "amused and watchful" air (Octave Maus), then gave a talk on "The Influence on Literature." Three years later this lecture would open Gide's volume of *Prétextes;* the last paragraphs of "The Influence," concerning 'Responsibility', contain the essential ideas of later works by Gide.

Instead of concerts there were poetry recitations, with poems sung to illustrate the lecture of Tristan Klingsor.

Chausson had died tragically the preceeding year.

(See Léo Jo: *La Libre Esthétique,* No. 42)

Maus, pp. 241-254.

6. LA LIBRE ESTHÉTIQUE (GATHERING FRUIT). 1901

Lithograph in orange, green and bistre.

74.0 × 43.0 cm.

Gisbert Combaz; lith. O. De Rycker & Mendel, Bruxelles. The text, at bottom, reads: La Libre Esthétique Salon Annuel: Musée Moderne: de 10 à 5 H [eure]s, Ouverture: 1ier Mars, Prix d'entrée: 1 fr., le dimanche, 50 c.
Coll. W.D. No. 48.

The first paintings of Vuillard and *l'Inondation* by Monet astounded the visitors to the 1901 Salon of *La Libre Esthétique.* A still-life by Cézanne and *Hommage à Cézanne* by Maurice Denis were denounced by the critics; Cross was more than misunderstood; Lemmen showed a new style; Van Rysselberghe enlarged his brushstroke.

Henri Ghéon, who had returned with André Gide from the Sahara, gave a lecture on "Poetry and Empiricism." There was a performance of the Schola Cantorum, founded in 1900 by Vincent d'Indy, Charles Bordes and Alexandre Guilmant.

Maus, pp. 255-266.

7. LA LIBRE ESTHÉTIQUE (HARVESTING SUNFLOWERS). 1902

Lithograph in yellow, flesh, light blue, medium blue, black and violet.

60.0 × 44.5 cm.

A print without text; in the poster, the text is located below the design. G.C.; lith. O. De Rycker & Mendel, Bruxelles.
Coll. W.D. No. 50.

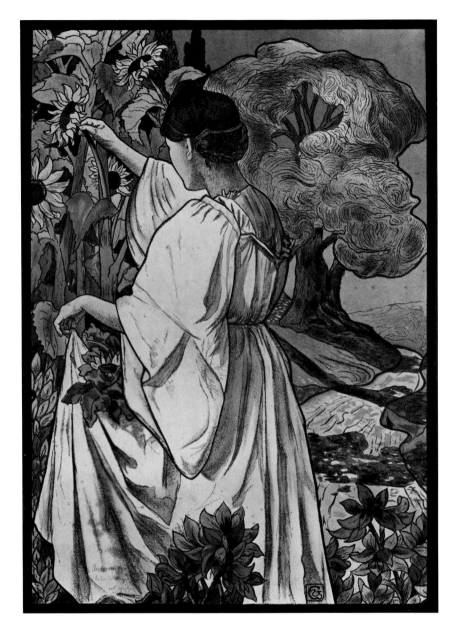

"I have such good memories of the happy days we spend in Brussels! We will bring our suit-cases full of enthusiasm (Maus, p. 283) . . . Ah! the joy . . . the enthusiasm, how good it is! How wonderful it is to love, to love all that is Beautiful and Good!" (p. 284). Thus did Blanche Selva write to Octave Maus, expressing a feeling shared by many of those in *La Libre Esthétique*—the importance of friendship, and of rigorous work as well:

> "The new musical works give rise to un-expected interpreters and virtuosity is de-veloping at the same time that art is evolving. When Dukas' sonata appeared last year, one wondered what pianist would dare accept the challenge. Edouard Risler played it trium-phantly at the *Société nationale,* and now there is an 18-year-old girl who in turn interprets it masterfully before an enthusiastic audience at *La Libre Esthétique.* This young woman is Miss Blanche Selva. . ." (p. 280)

An exceptionally gifted pianist, Blanche Selva was a disciple of Vincent d'Indy and was already, at age eighteen, a professor at the Schola Cantorum. On Sunday afternoons she would bring together at her Paris home the best musicians of the day:

> "Ah! those Sundays at Miss Selva's, what delights and what lessons! D'Indy would lis-ten, while turning the pages, to a rendition of the *Baigneuses au Soleil* by Severac; and Severac himself would be amazed by the sense of gushing water, of sparkling light, that the interpreter could draw forth. Albeniz experi-enced the same delight listening to the twelve pieces of *Iberia.* Dukas **placed** on the piano his *Variations sur un thème de Rameau;* Breville, his short score of *Stamboul;* Roussel, his *Evoca-tions.* And so it went in this circle of friends, united by the same artistic ideal, by the inti-macy of the too-short hours spent in the love of music and the admiration of she who brought it to them." (p. 280)

Similar gatherings were arranged in Brussels, and Blanche Selva faithfully attended the meetings of

La Libre Esthétique for eleven consecutive years.

It was also a great year for lecturers: Adrien Mithouard defined "The Classics of Tomorrow"; Georgette Leblanc spoke about "Women in the Theater."

In the field of art, the friends of Toulouse-Lautrec, who had died the previous year, paid homage to his memory with an exhibition. Rodin showed his *Bourgeois de Calais;* Vallotton sent woodcut portraits of Baudelaire and Dostoevsky;

Charles Guérin showed the *Jardin aux roses* (later purchased by André Gide). Octave Maus espe-cially liked the "soft, airy, brightly colored" pastel drawings by Alexander Robinson, an American painter living in Bruges at the time. Robinson wrote to Maus: "I am delighted that you will have one of my pastels and I hope *Lysabetta* will keep my memory 'green' with you." And it did. (p. 272).

Maus, pp. 267-284.

8. LA LIBRE ESTHÉTIQUE (HARBOUR). 1903

Lithograph in yellow, orange, light purple, dark purple, blue and black.

74.0 × 43.0 cm.

G.C.; lith. O. De Rycker & Mendel, Bruxelles.
Coll. W.D. No. 56.

This poster was shown at the 1903 Salon.

1903 was a year of recapitulation: it was the 10th anniversary of *La Libre Esthétique*. Their expositions since 1893 had included 425 exhibitors, 43 lectures, 27 concerts of mostly unpublished works.

Paul Du Bois and Gisbert Combaz organized a celebration in honor of Maus. They gathered together 150 pieces by artists who had exhibited at *La Libre Esthétique*—a collection Maus would later offer to the Ixelles museum.

1903 was a musical year, teeming with new works by Belgian composers, among them Joseph Jongen. Maus gave a lecture-concert on "Humor in Music"; he often participated directly in the concerts, and showed himself to be an accomplished pianist. Eugene Ysaÿe discussed with him the possibility of founding a "Belgian Society of Modern Music," to fill a need which the large symphonic concerts could only meet in part. "To found the 'Thursday symphonies', where only experimental pieces—nothing but new and mainly Belgian works—would be played, would be an undertaking that I feel I could direct, but not organize. You alone can do it, my dear Octave." (Letter from Ysaÿe to Maus). But the project was never realized.

Maus, pp. 285-306.

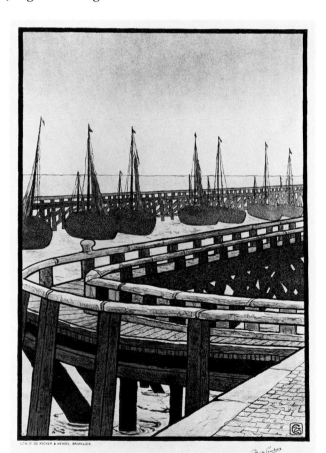

(Frontispiece)

9. LA LIBRE ESTHÉTIQUE (BOAT). 1906

Lithograph in yellow, bright red, light blue, dark gray and purple.

53.9 × 38.3 cm.

Gisbert Combaz; lith. O. De Rycker & Mendel, Bruxelles. The text, at bottom, reads: Musée moderne, Salon de la Libre Esthétique—22 février-25 mars, Entrée un franc.
Coll. W.D. No. 1509.

"... *Toute la mer va vers la ville!*
La mer pesante ardente et libre ...
La mer où les courants tracent les certitudes ..."
Emile Verhaeren, "Le port,"
(from *Les Villes Tentaculaires*, 1895)

"Evolution" was the theme of the 1906 Salon. Matisse, the sculptor Maillol, Lucie Cousturier—none of the exhibitors had participated in previous exhibitions (except Isidor Verheyden, who had died 1 November 1905 and was represented by works not previously exhibited). Van Dongen was invited but would participate at a later date.

In the preface to the catalogue Maus stated that "the victories of impressionism being assured, the dominant concerns have changed their focus. Many try to bring art back to the simple sources of emotion ... The analytic principle gives way to the synthetic method."

Fauré, Director of the Paris Conservatory, took part in the concerts. The ambiance was often tender, often mischevious.

Maus, pp. 349-364.

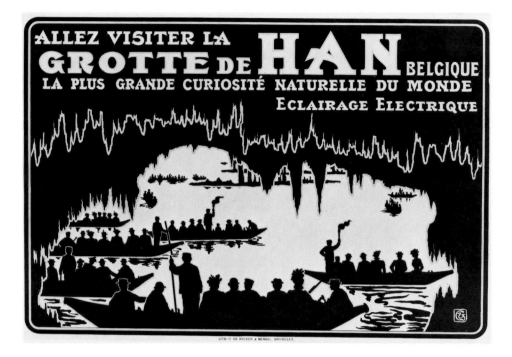

10. GROTTE DE HAN. Undated

Lithograph in yellow, orange and black.

43.4 × 57.0 cm.

G.C.; lith. O. De Rycker & Mendel, Bruxelles.
Coll. W.D. No. 318.

11. À LA TOISON D'OR (EXPOSITIONS . . .) 1895

Lithographs in orange, blue and sky blue.

47.3 × 30.6 cm.

Gisbert Combaz 1895; no printer's name.
Coll. W.D. No. 34.

The *Maison d'Art "À la Toison d'Or"* had about it a very special aura. As Maurice Bauwens explains in *Les Affiches Étrangères Illustrées* (Paris, 1897), the organizers reverently referred to it as "Madame la Maison d'Art."

The history of this firm, which was unique in Brussels at the time, began on 7 March 1894, when *S.A. l'Art* (Art Inc.) was incorporated in Brussels. In its statutes it had as its objective "the application of arts to industry in general, and their relevance to daily life . . ." An article in *L'Art Moderne* further explained that "the new society proposes to become the intermediary between the buyers, the manufacturers and the artists.

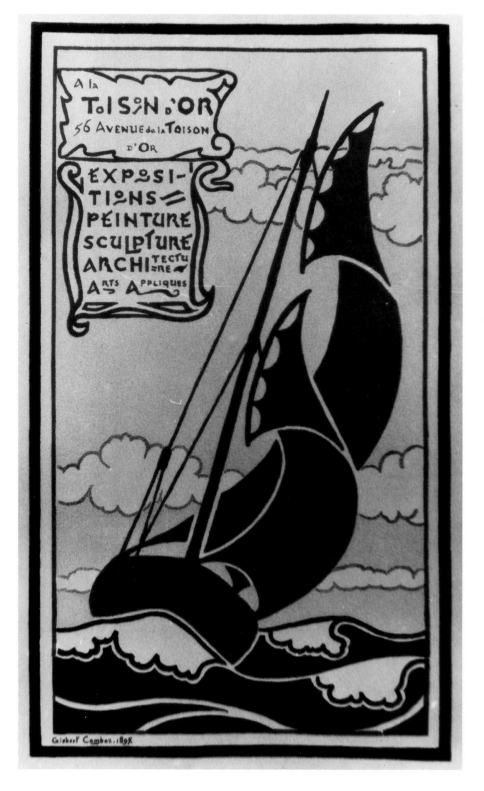

It has taken the anonymous form [of a corporation] because it wants to represent an idea and not personalities: it has taken a commercial form because without capital it would never be considered as a force among the industrialists for whom it is designed.''

Among the founders were Edmond Picard, Octave Maus, Emile Verhaeren, a number of artists, several industrialists, and Charles Buls, the Mayor of Brussels and the president of the Association for the Progress of Decorative Arts. Towards the end of 1894 the *S.A. l'Art* moved its headquarters to 56, avenue de la Toison d'Or, the former residence of Edmond Picard, where it officially opened in early 1895 under the direction of Picard's son, William. The intimate atmosphere of a private residence proved ideal for giving exposure both to works of art and to new ideas: the artistic fervor and hospitality that flourished there gave birth to great retrospectives (Laermans, Rodin, A.J. Heymans, Verhaeren, French and Belgian posters), concerts, lectures, and avant-garde theater plays, as well as a series of philosophical pamphlets.[1]

The *Maison d'Art* closed six or seven years after its opening, but its role was significant. It had responded so well to a crucial question of the time—how to reconcile art and industry—that S. Bing, intrigued by the same question, would be inspired to transform his Paris store into a similar organization.

(See Combaz: *Premier Congrès International des Avocats*, No. 1; and keep in mind the efforts of *La Libre Esthétique*, which were taking place at the same time.)

[1]According to a list found in pamphlet No. 7 in this series, the titles of the pamphlets were: (1) À la Toison d'Or: Une maison d'Art à Bruxelles; (2) Notice sur la Maison d'Art; (3) Madame la Maison d'Art; (4) Comment vivra la Maison d'Art; (5) Dividendes Intellectuels; (6) Pour qui il faut posséder les oeuvres d'Art; (7) La Socialisation de l'Art; and (8) Le Théâtre de la Maison d'Art.

Anonymous, ''La société anonyme 'L'Art' '' in *L'Art Moderne*, Brussels, No. 10, 11 March 1894, pp. 78-79; Anonymous, ''Concours pour un projet de mobilier de chambre à coucher,'' *op. cit.*, No. 27, 8 July 1894, p. 217; Anonymous, '' 'À la Toison d'or,' Une maison d'Art à Bruxelles,'' *op. cit.*, 16 December 1894, pp. 395-397; Anonymous, ''À la Maison d'Art, Exposition d'affiches françaises et belges,'' *op. cit.*, 17 May 1896, p. 157; Edmond Picard, ''Exposition de l'oeuvre de A.-J. Heymans à la Maison d'Art de Bruxelles,'' *op. cit.*, 21 January 1900, pp. 17-19; F.J., ''La Maison d'Art,'' *op. cit.*, 22 July 1900, p. 233; Maus, p. 200.

12. THREE POSTERS FOR LA MAISON D'ART ''À LA TOISON D'OR'' Undated

From a series of eight lithographs printed in different hues on papers of various textures and colors. Coll. W.D. No. 5423/A: orange background, blue ship and somber green waves on thick white paper; Coll. W.D. No. 5423/C: red background, black ship and blue waves on cream-colored paper; Coll. W.D. No. 5423/E: monochromatic red on white paper showing a partial watermark, ''. . . nal Turkey Mill Kent.''

Each design measures 35.1 × 25.0 cm.

Each with the initials G.C.

''. . . Et leur barque ostentatoire et colossale
s'érige, au carrefour des cent routes paradoxales . . .''

Emile Verhaeren, ''La Joie'' (from *Les Visages de la Vie*, 1899)

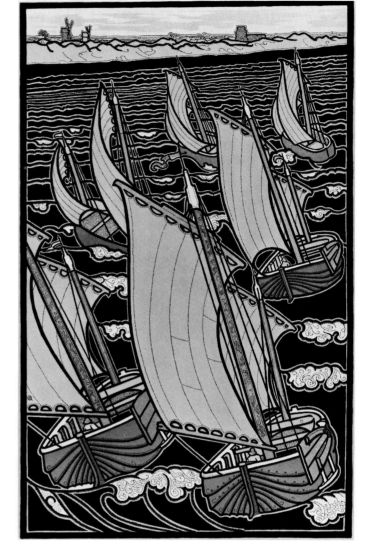

13. FLEET OF FISHING BOATS. 1899

Lithograph in yellow, gray, blue-gray, green, red and black. From a series that includes Nos. 14, 15 and 16.

48.7 × 41.5 cm.

G.C.; éditeurs Dietrich & Co., Bruxelles, imprimé par O. De Rycker & Mendel, Bruxelles.
Coll. W.D. No. 965.

The original pen-and-ink drawings for this and for *Le Moulin* (No. 15) were exhibited at *La Libre Esthétique* in 1899; they were reproduced in *l'Art Décoratif* (no. 7, p. 33) along with two other drawings from the same series having religious themes.

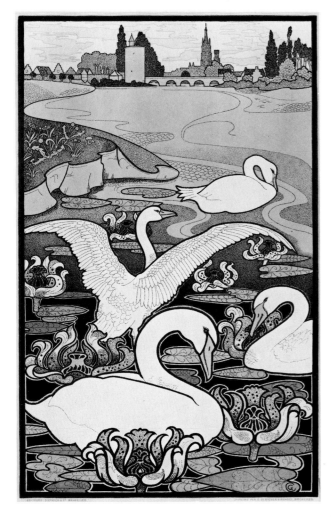

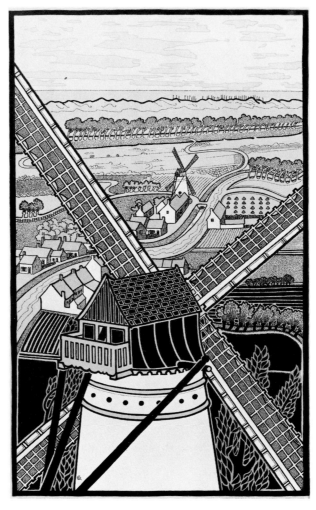

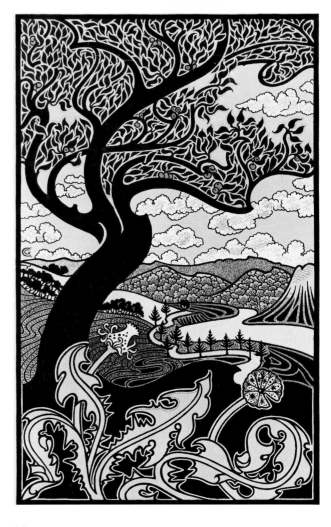

14. SWANS AT BRUGES. 1899

Lithograph in yellow, gray, blue-gray, green, red and black.

48.7 × 31.5 cm.

G.C.; éditeurs Dietrich & Co., Bruxelles; imprimé par O. De Rycker & Mendel, Bruxelles.

Coll. W.D. No. 963.

> *"O mai! moment blanc de l'année!*
> *Mois des blancs unanimes,*
> *Des blancs—comme neigés!*
> *Blancs des jardins et des vergers*
> *Blanc des cygnes,*
> *Blancs unanimes! . . .*
>
>   *   *   *
>
> *Les cygnes ont ouvert leur aile*
> *En forme de harpes*
> *Harpes de Lohengrin aux musiques d'argent."*
>   Georges Rodenbach, "Le miroir du ciel natal"

15. LE MOULIN. 1899

Lithograph in yellow, gray, blue-gray, green, red and black.

48.7 x 31.5 cm.

G.C.; éditeurs Dietrich & Co., Bruxelles; imprimé par O. De Rycker & Mendel, Bruxelles.

Coll. W.D. No. 964.

The pen-and-ink drawing for this print was reproduced in an article by Octave Maus, "Les Industries d'Art au Salon de La Libre Esthétique" (A & D, January-June 1899, vol. 5, p. 101).

16. LANDSCAPE WITH TREE. 1899

Lithograph in yellow, gray, blue-gray, green, red and black.

48.7 x 31.5 cm.

G.C., éditeurs Dietrich & Co., Bruxelles; imprimé par O. De Rycker & Mendel, Bruxelles.

Coll. W.D. No. 962.

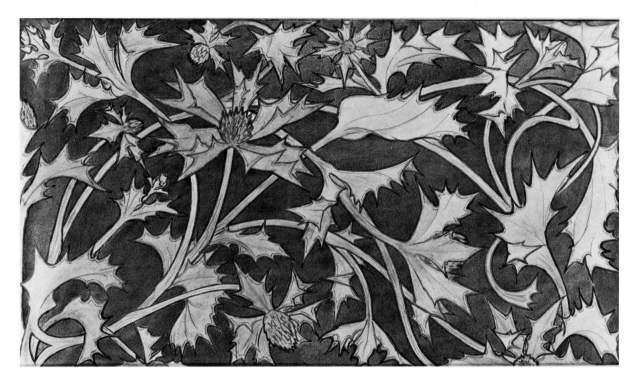

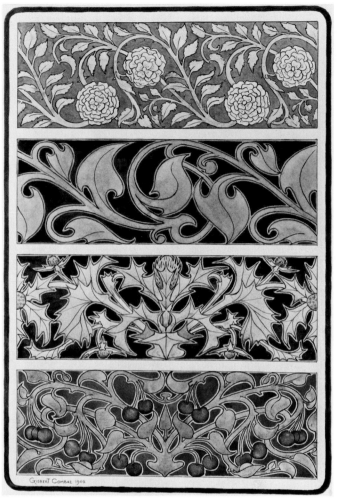

17. FRIEZE DESIGN: THISTLES. 1904

Gouache on drawing paper.

27.5 x 47.5 cm.

G.C., 1904
Coll. W.D. No. 5413.

18. FRIEZE DESIGN: HOLLY. Undated

Gouache on drawing paper.

27.8 × 45.3 cm.

Unsigned.
Coll. W.D. No. 5405.

19. FRIEZE DESIGN: FOUR PLANTS. 1902

Gouache on drawing paper.

10.0 x 28.3 cm. each element; outer dimensions of complete work: 46.1 x 31.0 cm.

Gisbert Combaz. 1902.
Coll. W.D. No. 5401.

20. FRIEZE DESIGN: FOUR PLANTS, AT RIGHT ANGLES. 1902

Gouache on drawing paper.

10.3 and 14.2 × 23.3 cm. each element.

Unsigned.
Coll. W.D. No. 5403.

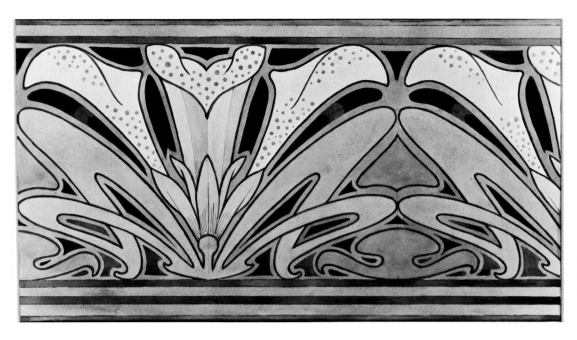

21. FRIEZE DESIGN: LILIES. Undated
Gouache on drawing paper.
25.8 x 45.5 cm.
Unsigned.
Coll. W.D. No. 5408.

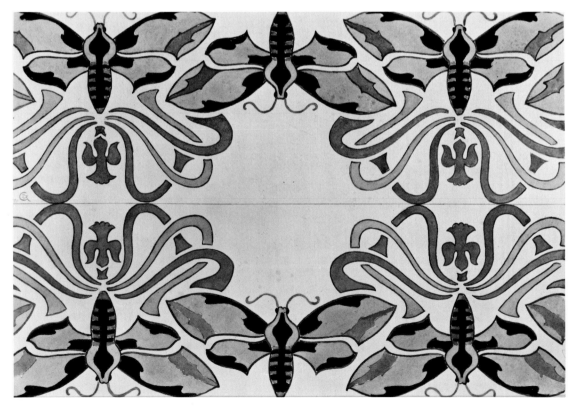

22. FRIEZE DESIGN: BUTTERFLIES. 1897
Gouache on drawing paper.
34.0 x 48.0 cm.
G.C. 1897.
Coll. W.D. No. 5411.

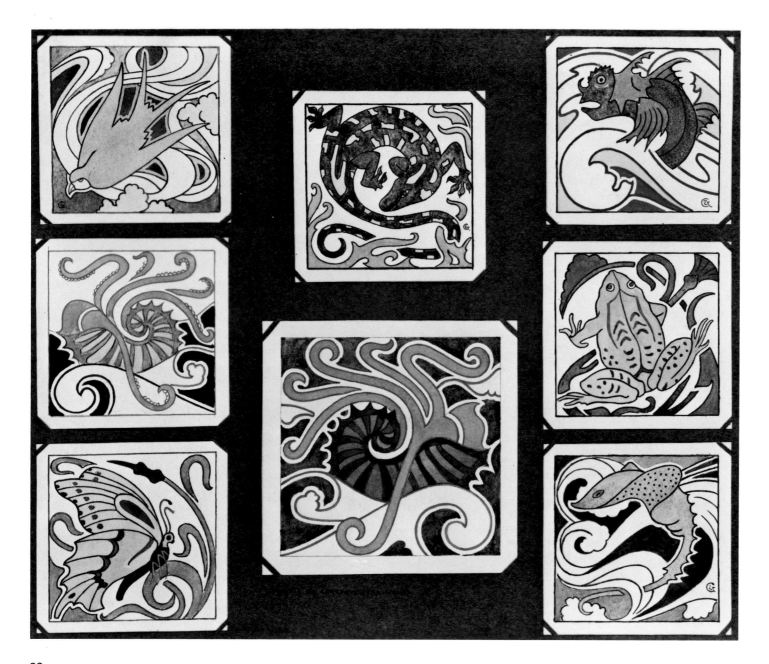

23. EIGHT MODELS FOR CERAMIC TILES. Undated

Reading clockwise, from upper right: Red Fish, Frog, Blue Fish, Argonaut
(or Paper Nautilus) I, Butterfly, Argonaut (or Paper Nautilus) II, Swallow
and Salamander.

Gouache on paper.

13.0 x 13.0 cm., and 17.5 x 17.5 cm.

The Swallow, the Salamander, the Red Fish and the Blue Fish are
initialled G.C.
Coll. W.D. No. 5402.

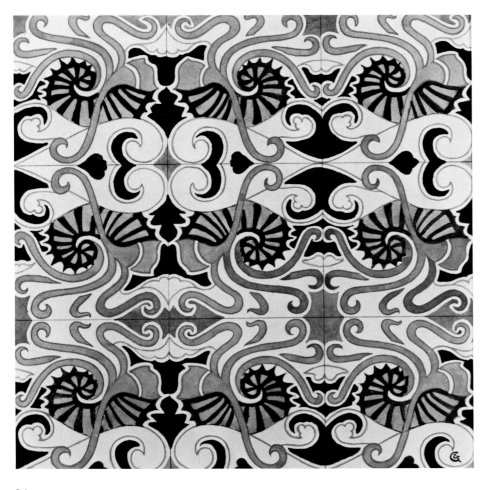

24. TILE DESIGN: LES ARGONAUTES. 1899

Gouache on paper.

11.3 x 11.3 cm. each tile; the project comprises nine tiles.

G.C.

Coll. W.D. No. 5414.

Here Combaz is again using, although with some variation, the "Argonaut" (or "Paper Nautilus") motif he had designed as the symbol for the *Maison d'Art* (see Y. Oostens-Wittamer, *Catalogue L'Affiche belge, 1892–1914,* Brussels, 1975, p. 140).

The tiles were made by Emile Müller d'Ivry and showed vigorous relief. The original drawings of the designs were reproduced in an article by Octave Maus, "Les industries d'Art au Salon de la Libre Esthétique" (A & D, Jan.–June 1899, vol. 5, p. 100).

25. TILE DESIGN: BUTTERFLIES. 1898

Gouache on pasteboard.

11.2 × 11.2 cm. each tile; the project comprises nine tiles.

G.C.

Coll. W.D. No. 5415.

This design was exhibited at the 1898 Salon of *La Libre Esthétique,* as were Nos. 26 and 27. An article by Maus reveals that the actual tiles were made by a Monsieur Evaldre; the article reproduces this and the two following designs (Octave Maus, "Le salon de la Libre Esthétique," in *Art et Décoration,* Jan.-June 1898, vol. 3, pp. 97 and 102).

26. TILE DESIGN: SWALLOWS. 1898

Gouache on drawing paper.

11.1 × 11.1 cm. each tile; the project comprises nine tiles.

G.C.

Coll. W.D. No. 5407.

A & D, Jan.-June 1898, vol. 3, pp. 97, 102.

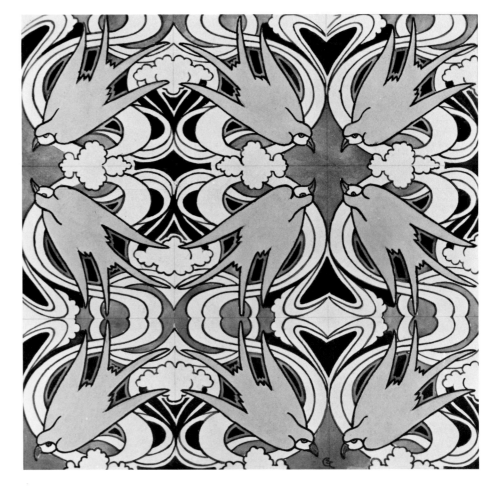

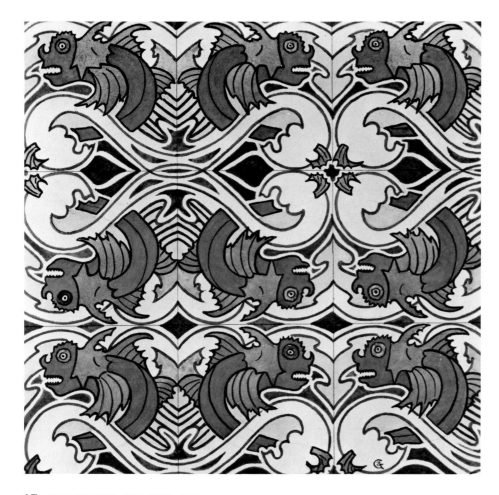

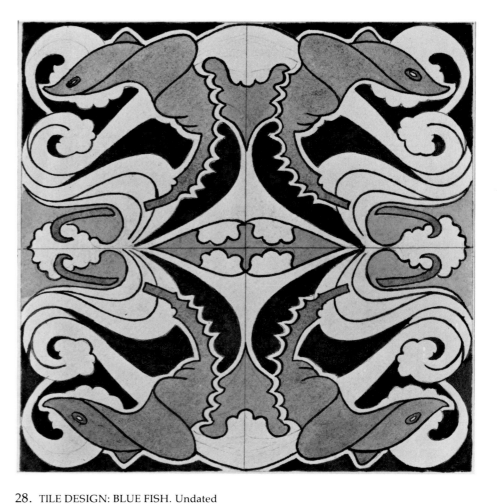

27. TILE DESIGN: RED FISH. 1898
Gouache on pasteboard.
11.1 × 11.1 cm. each tile; the project comprises nine tiles.
G.C.
Coll. W.D. No. 5412.
A & D, Jan.-June 1898, vol. 3, pp. 97, 102.

28. TILE DESIGN: BLUE FISH. Undated
Gouache on paper.
11.4 × 11.4 cm. each tile; the project comprises four tiles.
Unsigned.
Coll. W.D. No. 5417.

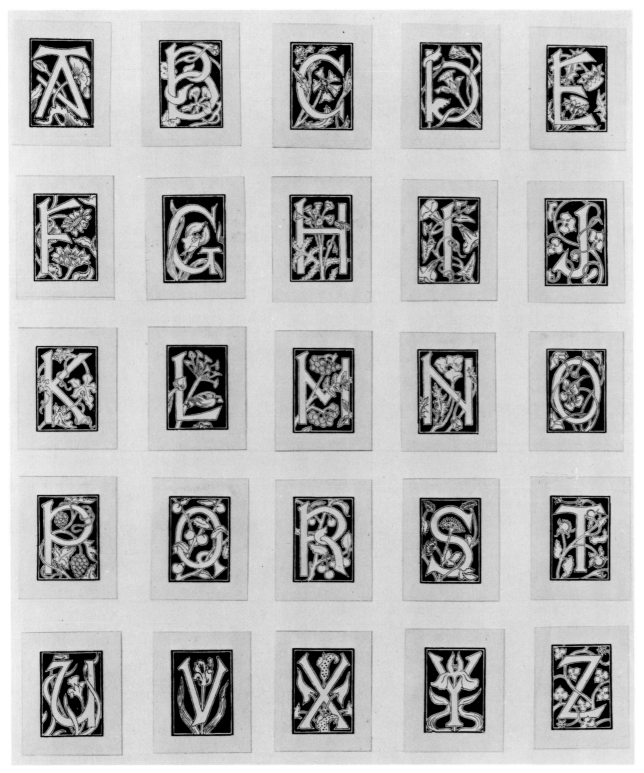

29. ORNAMENTAL ALPHABET. Undated

Black typography on white paper.

3.4 × 2.5 cm. each letter (A–Z, except W, which is omitted).

Unsigned.

Coll. W.D. No. 5406.

These ornamental letters were used in a 1906 issue of *Durendal* magazine (*Revue Catholique d'Art et de Littérature Durendal*, Brussels and Paris: Imprimerie Scientifique; Charles Bulens, editor). Combaz collaborated with *Durendal* on several occasions. One cover design bears the dedication, "To my dear, sweet fiancée, Gisbert, 5 April 1894" and shows a knight with sword in hand.

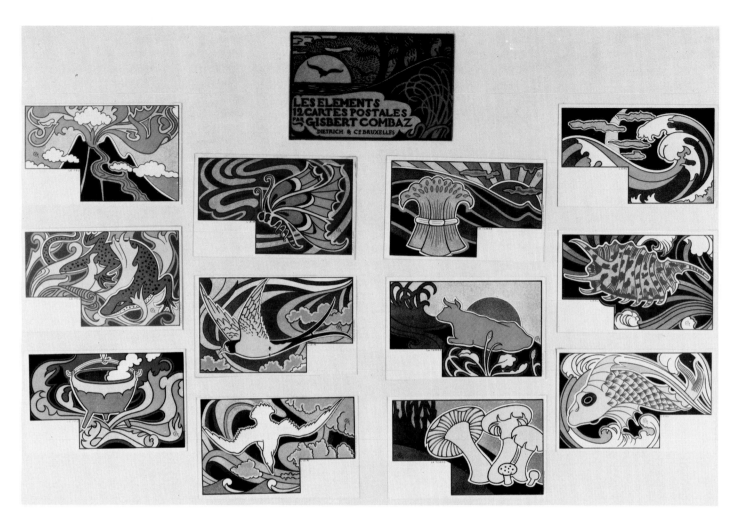

30. SERIES OF TWELVE POSTCARDS: LES ÉLÉMENTS
(L'AIR, L'EAU, LE FEU, LA TERRE). Undated

Lithographs in yellow, rose, red, light blue, dark blue, gray-mauve. The cover page is in light brown, dark brown and black.

9.0 × 14.0 cm.

G. C.; Dietrich & Co, Bruxelles (the cover page is inscribed with the full name, Gisbert Combaz).
Coll. W. D. No. 5425.

Reading from left to right, top to bottom, the designs are:
Col. I: LE FEU—Volcano, Salamander, Cauldron;
Col. II: L'AIR—Butterfly, Swallow, Gull; Col. III: LA TERRE—Sheaf of Wheat, Cow, Mushrooms; Col. IV: L'EAU—Wave, Sea Shell, Fish. Combaz designed another set of twelve postcards entitled *La Mer* (The Sea), which was also published by Dietrich & Co.

31. WAVE. 1901 (Illustrated on cover)

Gouache on heavy paper.

51.7 × 40.5 cm.

Gisbert Combaz, 1901.
Coll. W. D. No. 5001

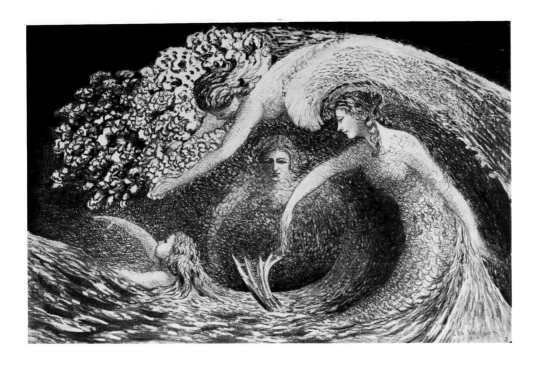

32. "LES VAGUES" 1916

Pencil and charcoal on paper.

50.0 × 74.9 cm.

Unsigned; Les vagues, 1916 I.
Coll. W. D. No. 5459.

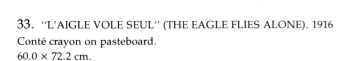

33. "L'AIGLE VOLE SEUL" (THE EAGLE FLIES ALONE). 1916

Conté crayon on pasteboard.

60.0 × 72.2 cm.

Gisbert Combaz, 1916. L'aigle vole seul. On the back of the frame, Combaz has written in ink: "Gisbert Combaz, 21 rue Seutin, Bruxelles, (Belgique). Exposition de Milan 1923." A numeral II is inscribed in orange pencil.
Coll. W. D. No. 5458.

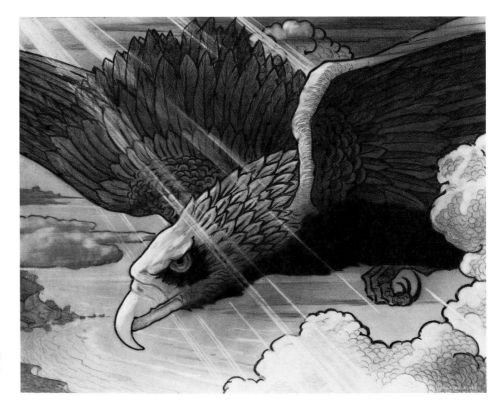

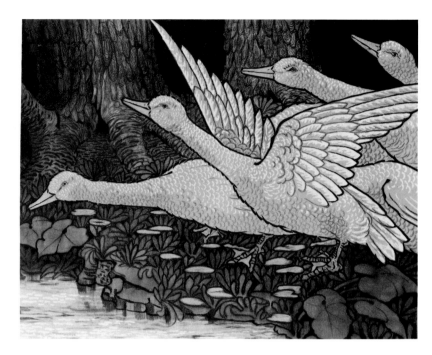

34. "ET LES OIES VONT EN BANDE" (AND THE GEESE DEPART IN A FLOCK). 1916

Drawing heightened with gouache, on beige pasteboard.

60.0 × 73.0 cm.

Gisbert Combaz 1916; Et les oies vont en bande. On the back of the frame the artist has written in ink: "Gisbert Combaz, 21 rue Seutin, Bruxelles (Belgique). Exposition de Milan 1923." A numeral III is inscribed in orange pencil.
Coll. W.D. No. 5457.

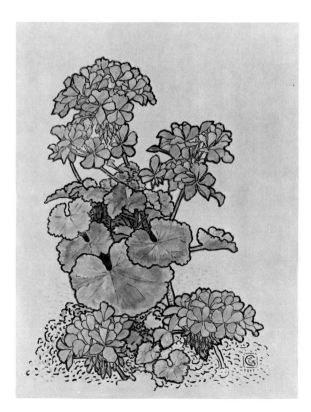

35. GERANIUMS. 1911
Gouache on pasteboard.
60.0 × 44.6 cm.
G.C. 1911.
Coll. W.D. No. 5449.

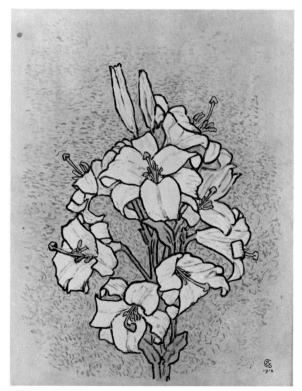

36. LILIES. 1912
Gouache on pasteboard.
60.0 × 44.6 cm.
G.C. 1912
Coll. W.D. No. 5448.

37. ORCHIDS AND BUTTERFLY. 1912

Gouache on pasteboard.

44.6 × 60.0 cm.

G.C. 1912.

Coll. W.D. No. 5451.

Man has long been fascinated by orchids, and literature abounds with references to their beauty, variety and mystery. In an article entitled "The Exquisite Orchids," Luis Marden points out that these plants are indigenous to every continent and flourish in myriad climates. He is amazed at the variety of their forms and colors—"Some of them mimic bees, wasps, butterflies, or moths; some resemble swans or doves; others look like frogs or lizards, or miniature men . . ." (Marden, p. 485-486), as well as their sizes—"the smallest . . . could fit in a thimble, and the largest . . . reaches a hundred feet" (ibid.).

Their perfumes are equally varied: "Depending on the species, the perfume evokes hyacinth, Russian leather, goats, spoiled meat, creosote, lilies, violets, etc. . . ." (Balis and Lawalrée, p. 11).

Because of their diversity, they attract a variety of insects, much to the delight of scientists and scholars. In his *Intelligence des Fleurs* (Paris, 1907), Maurice Maeterlinck devoted twenty-five pages to the subject of orchid fertilization. Charles Darwin, too, was fascinated by the various methods of pollinization and their implications, and in 1862 he published "The various contrivances by which orchids are fertilised by insects." Intrigued by one white orchid in Madagascar in which nectar was located at the very bottom of a foot-long spur, he deduced the existence of a large moth with an extremely long proboscis. His colleagues were incredulous; but forty years later the *Xanthopan morgani praedicta* was discovered in Madagascar—a nocturnal butterfly with a twelve-inch tongue (Marden, pp. 504, 505). And in Brussels, the entomologists at the Museum of Natural Science were always delighted to receive a shipment of orchids; over a two-year period, a careful inspection of newly arrived plants yielded more than 200 new varieties of insects (Balis and Lawalrée, p. 37).

Stories about orchids often intermingle fantasy with reality. According to Javanese mythology, the *Macodes petola (Lindl.)* (a small orchid with especially beautiful leaves) sprang from the silken threads of the veil of a lovely goddess who visited earth to help mankind. But she was rudely received and retreated in dismay to her home in the heavens, despite the pleas of some faithful followers who belatedly recognized her divinity. From the threads of her veil, which caught on the rocks as she fled, sprang up beautiful flowers that at first withered but later came back to life, indicating that the goddess had forgotten her rancor. And to this day an orchid with foliage like golden silk can be found in the heart of the Javanese forests (Balis and Lawalrée, pp. 10, 11).

(See Combaz: *Orchids*, No. 38; Livemont: *Michiels Fres. Pépiniéristes*, No. 103.)

Jan Balis and André Lawalrée, *L'orchidée en Belgique*, Bibliothèque Albert I, Brussels, July/September, 1961; Luis Marden, "The Exquisite Orchids," *National Geographic Magazine*, Washington, April 1971, pp. 484–513.

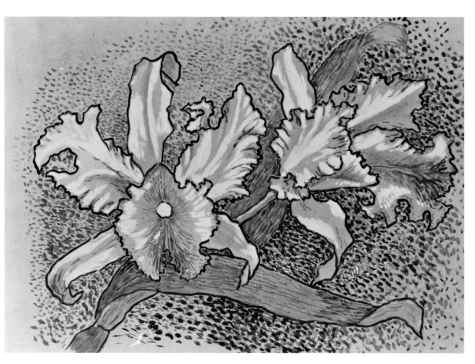

38. ORCHIDS. Undated

Gouache on pasteboard.

44.6 × 60.0 cm.

Unsigned.

Coll. W.D. No. 5452.

Jean Linden, a doctor, explorer, horticulturist and botanist who was known as the "father of orchids," is credited with having introduced at least 1,800 species of orchids into Belgium. In addition, he conducted research in methods of orchid cultivation and in 1845 founded in Brussels the *Horticulture Internationale*, the influence of which would extend to the United States and Russia.

The search for new varieties of orchids drew increasing attention during the 19th century. Plant hunters would traverse the globe, braving both natural and political dangers in order to bring back abundant supplies of the exotic plants, which would then be sold for spectacular prices: before the end of the century one English firm would employ 140 such persons (Simon, p. 14). The methods used to gather specimens were unregulated and often resulted in the destruction of plants, leading a number of tropical countries around 1890 to outlaw such harvesting (Balis, p. 62; Whittle, pp. 10, 11).

The public's infatuation with the flowers was sustained and encouraged by the publication of extraordinarily beautiful lithographs; many of these were gathered together by Jan Balis to make rich, vibrant catalogues.

In 1892 horticulturists at last succeeded in reproducing orchids from seeds—the result of thirteen years of experimentation by Charles Vuylsteke, who in 1904 received the Royal Horticultural Society's gold medal at the London Temple Show (Balis, pp. 62, 63). Subsequent discoveries by the Frenchman Noel Bernard and the American, Dr. Lewis Knudson, led to a simple method of orchid culture that was employed until 1956, when it was replaced by the meristematic method of the Frenchman Georges Morel (Marden, p. 489).

(See also Combaz: *Orchids and Butterfly*, No. 37.)

Jan Balis, *Hortus Belgicus,* Bibliothèque Albert I, Brussels, August-September 1962; Peter McKenzie Black, *Beautiful orchids,* London, 1973; Lucien Linden, A. Cosniaux, G. Grisman, *Les Orchidées exotiques et leur culture en Europe,* Brussels and Paris, 1894; Hilda Simon, *The private lifes of orchids,* Philadelphia and New York, 1976; Tyler Whittle, *The Plant Hunters,* London, 1970.

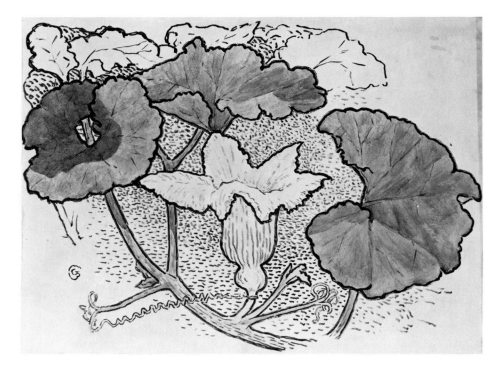

39. COLOCYNTH. Undated
Gouache on pasteboard.
44.6 × 60.0 cm.
G.C.
Coll. W.D. No. 5450.

40. WISTARIA. 1911(?)
Gouache on pasteboard.
44.6 × 60.0 cm.
G.C. 1911 or 1914.
Coll. W.D. No. 5453.

GISBERT COMBAZ, ARTIST AND ORIENTALIST

Let me leave it to others, better qualified than I, to emphasize what his passion for the Orient brought to the art of Gisbert Combaz. Instead, I shall stress the influence of his artistic experience upon his scholarly pursuits.

On the one hand, Combaz' aesthetic sensitivity is apparent in all his writings. For this pioneer in the history of art, venturing beyond the borders of Europe, a document is always more than just a document. His artist's eye reinforces the eye of the scholar and allows him to see more clearly. On the other hand, his technical expertise enables him to illustrate most of his own work. His drawings of decorative motifs and of buildings are bold and competent: more effectively than photography, they reveal the essential characteristics. In his most successful drawings one feels that the hand of the sixty-year-old Combaz has not lost the skill it had in youth, when at the turn of the century he made such beautiful posters.

His first scholarly works date only from the end of the period known as *La Belle Époque: The Imperial Burial Grounds of China* (1907), *The Imperial Palaces of China* (1909), *The Imperial Temples of China* (1912), published by the enterprising Brussels art publisher, Vromant, who was to do so much to promote interest in Oriental art. With the advent of a very unstable republic in China, the imperial city of Peking (which had so stimulated the imagination of his fellow artist, Victor Segalen, who was both scholar and explorer) ceased to be the "forbidden city." Today it is the superb architecture of the imperial palaces in Peking that is most often shown to visitors. There is no book on the subject. Is it not time for a new edition of Combaz' works?

In 1929 the Institute for Advanced Chinese Studies, still very much alive today, was founded in Brussels. It straightway sponsored a prestigious publication: *Mélanges Chinois et Bouddhiques,* hereafter referred to as MCB. Gisbert Combaz devoted himself to this task with exemplary zeal.

In this context he first published *l'Évolution du Stūpa en Asie,* as a series of articles. Each was distinguished for its thoroughgoing focus on a question concerning which, at this period, individual discoveries and interpretations abounded. His first contribution was entitled "Étude d'Architecture Bouddhique" (MCB II [1933] pp. 163-305); the second was "Contributions nouvelles et vue d'ensemble" (MCB III [1935] pp. 93-144), and the third, "Les Symbolismes du Stūpa" (MCB IV [1936] pp. 1-125.)

L'Évolution du Stūpa en Asie in fact formed the appendix of a more general work, *l'Inde et l'Orient Classique,* which remained unpublished until it appeared as the first volume in the series *Documents d'Art et d'Archéologie* (Published by the Musée Guimet, Paris, 1937), thanks to his friendship with René Grousset and Joseph Hackin.

Grousset, who took a predominantly historical approach (even though it is for his initiation into Indian philosophies that he is best remembered) certainly found a kindred spirit in Combaz, whose approach was essentially archeological. Using this archeological approach, Combaz defined his symbolic typology, which he called in his last work (MCB VII [1945] p. 230) a "philology of forms." The term is not very apt. Certainly the term used several years later by André Malraux, "physiology of art," would have been more appropriate. Malraux' work would have more sweep, and sometimes more genius, but also less soundness and more bathos. From Combaz' art—powerful, elegant and yet finely detailed—we know what to expect in his books: a method, a precision and also a large reservoir of knowledge, both artistic and literary. He does not seem to have been able to read Asian languages, but he was apparently familiar with all of the many translations into Western languages that appeared in his day. With Paul Pelliot, whose help he sometimes acknowledged, he shared an abundance of information, extending from Egypt, Greece and Early Asia, to as far as Indonesia and Japan, if not covering pre-Columbian America. Combaz does not seem to have followed in the footsteps of Richard Hentze, his colleague at the Belgian Institute for Advanced Chinese Studies. On the contrary, one gets the feeling that another colleague from the same institution, Louis de La Vallée Poussin, whose caution verged on a methodical skepticism, left his mark on Combaz' writings. As of all pioneers, one can say of Combaz that he died too soon in 1941; many of the archeological discoveries that took place in China and in Soviet Central Asia during the latter half of the twentieth century would have served to reinforce certain of his cautious hypotheses.

"Asia is One" is a slogan coined at the beginning of this century by a Japanese esthete, Okakura Kakuzō (Tenshin), who would have been hard put to it to supply a solid basis for his intuition. While politically untrue, this intuition was nevertheless culturally valid; it is the theme of the cultural oneness of Asia that would be the conclusion reached in the final work of Gisbert Combaz, published posthumously, *Masques et Dragons en Asie* (MCB VII [1945] pp. 1-328). In this work he attacks the watertight compartments in which the principal Asian civilizations are confined, concluding that their inter-relationship is far greater than one had believed. Was it not first Moslem and then Western imperialism, which, in defining its zones of influence, isolated the Asiatic countries from each other?

As René Grousset and Jeannine Auboyer state so well in the

obituary which prefaces the posthumous work of Combaz, his *magnum opus* may be thought of as a triptych, in which *L'Inde et l'Orient Classique* occupies the center panel, while the studies— one architectural and religious (the *Stūpa*), and the other, decorative and symbolic *(Masques et Dragons)*—constitute the wings.

By comparison with these major works his reflective study, *La Peinture Chinoise vue par un Peintre Occidental,* MCB VI [1939] pp. 11-149, is far more dated. In this he is too indebted to *Kiai-tseu-yuan houa tchouan* (Garden as large as a mustard seed), Paris, Renouard, 1918—a translation, very commendable for that period, of a rather belated treatise on painting. Its translator was the Chinese scholar and art lover, Raphaël Petrucci, with whom Combaz must certainly have been well acquainted in Brussels. After Combaz' death, on the one hand, specifically the work of R.B. Acker (professor first at Leyden, then at Ghent), of Erik Zürcher (professor at Leyden), and of Pierre Ryckmans (doctor of the University of Louvain, professor at Hong Kong and later, Camberra) served to renew our knowledge of Chinese esthetics. On the other hand, the sensational discoveries of ancient mural paintings in China served to invalidate the gloomy forebodings of Combaz.

There is no doubt that he would have made full use of this new evidence, just as, with impressive modesty and discipline, he knew how to revise his theories on Buddhist art in the light of new information that came to him during the Golden Age of Indian, Serindian, Indochinese and Indonesian archeology.

HUBERT DURT
Member of l'École Française d'Extrême-Orient
Editor of *Hōbōgirin* (French dictionary
of Buddhist Sino-Japanese terminology.)

LÉO JO (LÉONTINE JORIS)
(Tournai 1870 - Brussels 1962)

Caricaturist, poster designer, painter, creator of children's toys

"I just don't understand! If you want to be an artist you must have a name, and when the name you have taken begins to be known, so much the better! If not, you would have to change it every six months. . .moreover, you would be recognized anyway." Thus wrote Octave Maus to his good friend Léo Jo. Léo Jo was a charming, petite young lady, with brown hair pulled back in a chignon, bright, sparkling eyes that moved with a disconcerting rapidity, and a joyous laugh always ready to burst forth. Cultivated and witty, she was also very modest. A letter from Ray Nyst (April 23, 1914) is as significant as the one from Maus: Nyst had asked her—in vain—for biographical and technical information for the artists' directory, *L'Annuaire des Artistes*. "If I am treating you a little roughly, it is because I am annoyed that a sharp mind like yours is content to answer, 'I have nothing to say.'"

Jo was the daughter of a doctor. Even as a young child she could not resist caricaturing her surroundings. One day her father showed her sketches to the sculptor Van der Stappen who, charmed by them, had her come to see him so that he might encourage her. However, he refused to give her regular lessons for fear of stifling her talent.

She instinctively saw the humor in a situation and searched for its inner meaning. She sketched her characters in a single creative stroke, harmoniously intermingling mass and detail. Her talent rejected bitterness: on the contrary, set-backs seemed rather to increase her sympathetic understanding.

Led by her inspiration and faithful to her motto, "Castigat ridendo mores," Léo Jo recorded the different stages of life, showing an equal affection for rich and poor, for their dreams, their pursuits, their customs. She knew how to give great breadth to her posters and drawings: her brushstroke was without pretension, yet had a lively intensity. In her works, attention was centered on the top portion: strong areas of color climbed upwards, supported at times by oblique axes. Clothing was used not to isolate her characters but rather to bring them closer to us.

Léo Jo went on to produce landscapes, still-lifes, and, in her later years, religious subjects. She became interested in book illustration and contributed to the illustration of Maurice des Ombiaux's *Contes de Sambre-et-Meuse* (Brussels, 1905) and *Les manches de lustrine* (Paris, 1913). For the benefit of World War I invalids she designed children's toys, including a set of nine-pins modeled after different characters.

Among the expositions in which she took part were *La Libre Esthétique* of 1899, 1900 and 1912; *la Société Nationale des Aquarellistes et Pastellistes de Belgique* (1903), the 10th International Venice Exposition (1912), and *Le Cercle Artistique et Littéraire de Bruxelles* (1928). Her caricatures were published in numerous periodicals, including *L'Art Décoratif* (Paris), *Comica* (Paris), *Le Rire* (Paris), *Le Samedi* (Brussels), *Simplicissimus* (Munich) and *L'Illustration Européenne* (Brussels).

Unedited artist's archives; unedited autobiographical childhood memories; communications from Mrs. W. Van Overstraete, niece of the artist; Maus, pp. 233, 234, 241, 435; Alfred Ruhemann, *Jung Belgien*, Berlin, n.d., p. 15.

41. POSTER DESIGN (?): "VITA BREVIS, RIDENTES EAMUS." Undated

Gouache on gray-beige paper.

75.5 × 37.0 cm.

Unsigned; Vita brevis, ridente [sic] eamus.
Coll. W.D. No. 2003

(Illustrated on page 6)

42. LA LIBRE ESTHÉTIQUE. 1900.

Lithograph in red, orange, green, black and violet. The violet is shaded off towards the top by diminishing the flow of ink.

155.0 × 81.0 cm.

Leo Jo; Affiches d'art O. De Rycker & Mendel, Bruxelles.
Coll. W.D. No. 127.

The monogram "LE" was created by Léo Jo for *La Libre Esthétique*. There is a poster by Combaz for the same salon (*La Libre Esthétique*, 1900) also printed by O. De Rycker (see No. 5). An instance of two posters being created for the same salon had occurred in 1896 and 1897, with one poster by Combaz and another by Van Rysselberghe, both printed by Vve Monnom. The reason for this is not known; perhaps it was a sign of enthusiasm, or was indicative of generosity on the part of the printers or patrons.

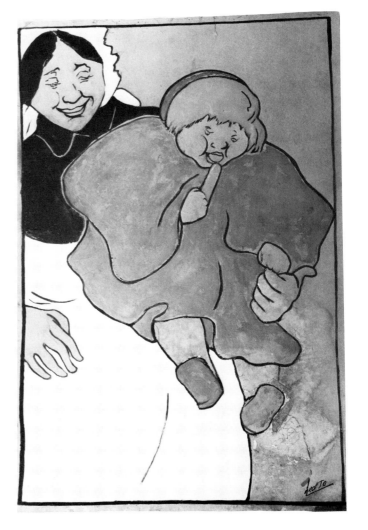

43. POSTER DESIGN: CHILD WITH COOKIE. Undated

Black, white, red and orange gouache on brown paper.

81.0 × 54.0 cm.

Leo Jo.
Coll. W.D. No. 2059.

This design appears in a photograph of Léo Jo in her studio.

(See also Léo Jo: *"De l'allure!"*, No. 66.)

Alfred Ruhemann, *Jung Belgien*, Berlin, n.d., p. 15.

44. "LÉANDRE." Undated

Gouache on drawing paper.

30.4 × 19.1 cm.

Léo Jo; Les félicitations! de Léandre à l'exposition des humoristes. Paris. Text written on the back in pencil.
Coll. W.D. No. 5781.

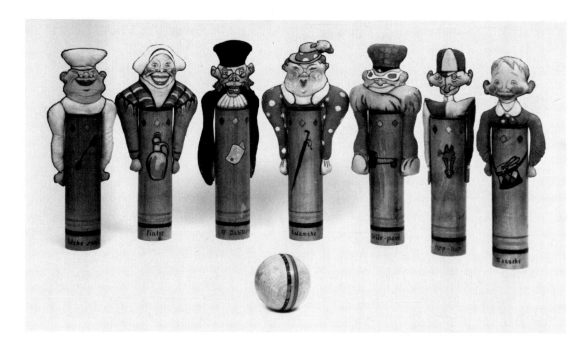

45. MODELS FOR TOYS: GAME OF NINEPINS. 1916-18

Wood and handpainted fabric.

Height: 38.5 cm.; diameter: 6.5 cm.

Leo Jo (signature painted on the base, slightly below each figure's left hand). Coll. W.D. No. 5780.

The game is composed of a wooden ball and seven ninepins representing different characters: *Madameke* and her umbrella (No. 1), *Lêche-Sauce* and his spoon (No. 2), *Fintje* and her pitcher (No. 3), *Mr. Babillard* and his papers (No. 4), *Hop-Hop* and his horse (No. 5), *Manneke* and his drum (No. 6), and *Brûle-Pavé* and his car (No. 7). Each ninepin is made of a wooden cylinder from which emerges the torso of the character, fashioned from hand-painted fabric. The wooden core is varnished; it bears the name of the character, plus his or her attribute, and it displays in two different ways the colors of the Belgian flag. A placement number can be found on the bottom of each pin. The adjustment of the paper patterns and the actual making up of the toys was entrusted to Fernande Dubois, an artist friend of Léo Jo's who was known for her tapestry weaving (from information supplied by Mme Van Overstraeten).

Léo Jo drew several models of toys for the cooperative society "Le Jouet Belge" (toys made by Belgian invalids and disabled war veterans), located at 24 rue d'Écosse in Brussels. Along with artists and students from professional schools, she produced cloth dolls (to be used as teapot covers) for an exhibition at the Ice Palace, under the patronage of the City of Brussels and with the approval of the National Committee for Food and Assistance.

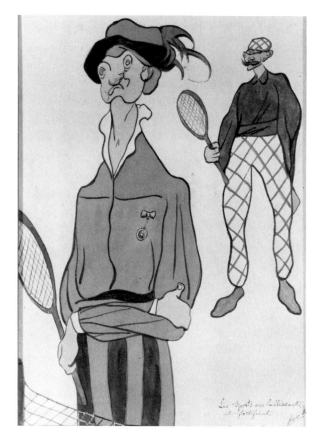

46. "LES SPORTS EMBELLISSENT ET FORTIFIENT" (SPORTS BEAUTIFY AND INVIGORATE"). Undated

Gouache on drawing paper, text in ink.

25.5 × 18.0 cm.

Léo Jo; Les sports embellissent et fortifient. Coll. W.D. No. 5711.

Reproduced in black and white in *Le Samedi* (Jan. 1899, p. 9) with a slightly modified text: "Sports beautify and invigorate. There are obvious links between Greek beauty and the Olympic Games."

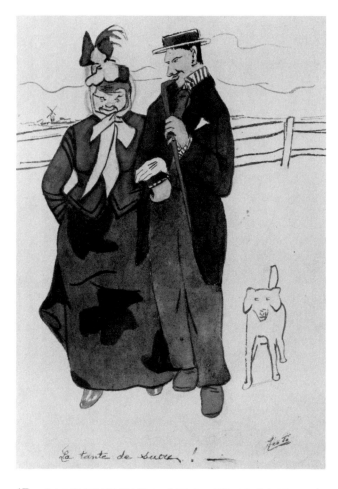

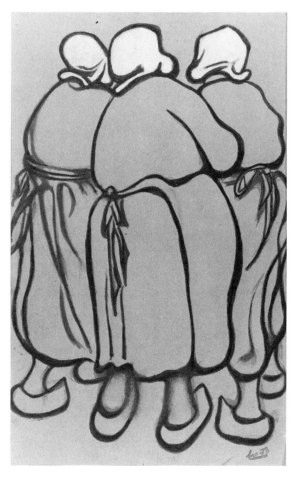

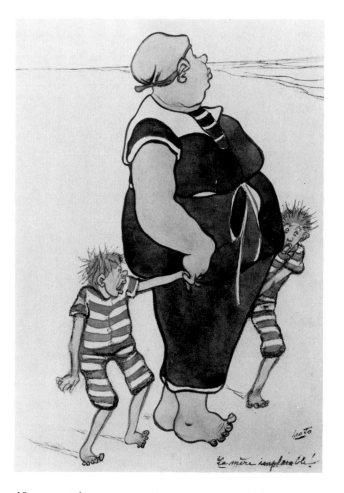

47. "LA TANTE DE SUCRE!" ("THE WELL-TO-DO AUNT!")
Undated

Gouache on drawing paper, text in ink.

25.5 × 17.5 cm.

Leo Jo; La tante de sucre!
Coll. W.D. No. 5753.

48. THREE WOMEN IN CLOGS,. Undated

Gouache on gray paper.

29.0 × 17.0 cm.

Leo Jo.
Coll. W.D. No. 5705.

49. "LA MÈRE IMPLACABLE!" ("THE IMPLACABLE
MOTHER!"). Undated

Gouache, ink and pencil on drawing paper.

26.2 × 18.0 cm.

Leo Jo; La mère implacable!
Coll. W.D. No. 5741.

50. BEACH SCENE. Undated

Gouache and pencil on drawing paper.

13.5 x 16.0 cm.

Léo Jo.
Coll. W.D. No. 5738.

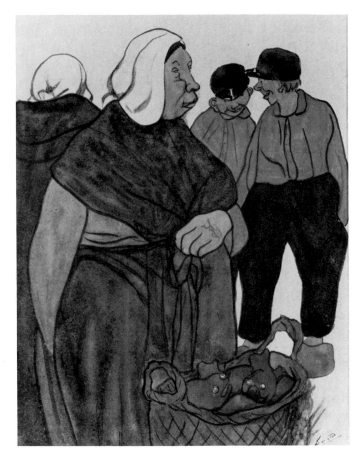

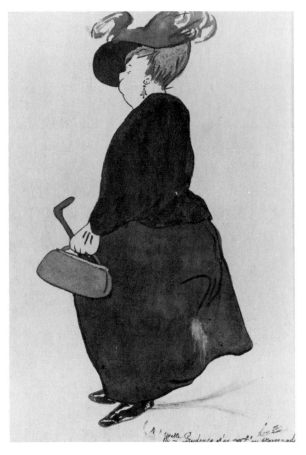

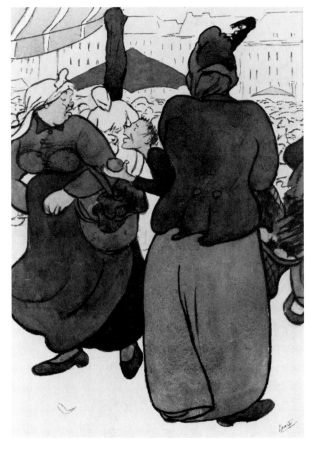

51. FISH VENDOR. Undated

Gouache on drawing paper.

24.5 x 18.0 cm.

Leo Jo.
Coll. W.D. No. 5739.

52. "MELLE PRUDENCE S'EN VA-T-EN PROMEN-
ADE" ("MISS PRUDENCE GOES FOR A STROLL").
Undated

Gouache on drawing paper; text in ink.

25.5 x 17.5 cm.

Leo Jo; Melle Prudence s'en va-t-en promenade.
Coll. W.D. No. 5732.

53. MARKET SCENE. Undated

Gouache on drawing paper.

23.0 x 16.0 cm.

Leo Jo.
Coll. W.D. No. 5729.

54. "GRAND PLACE, BRUXELLES." Undated

Gouache and pen on beige paper.

12.8 x 11.7 cm.

Leo Jo. The frame is inscribed in pencil: Gd Place Bruxelles.
Coll. W.D. No. 5713.

55. "LA POLICE AU GUET!" ("POLICE ON THE LOOK-
OUT!"). Undated

Gouache on drawing paper, text in ink.

26.0 x 18.0 cm.

Leo Jo; La police au guet!
Coll. W.D. No. 5728.

(Illustrated on page 6)

56. "LAQUELLE DES TROIS BUSES?" ("WHICH OF THE
    THREE TOP HATS?"). Undated

Gouache on drawing paper.

25.5 x 17.7 cm.

Léo Jo. Text written in ink on the back: Laquelle des trois buses?
(The French title plays upon the word "buse," which can mean
either "top hat" or "buzzard.")
Coll. W.D. No. 5716.

To the tune of the waltz, "Le Coeur de Ninon" (theme from the
Italian waltz, "Tesoro Mio"), music by E. Becucci and lyrics by
G. Millandy:

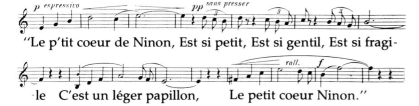

"Le p'tit coeur de Ninon, Est si petit, Est si gentil, Est si fragi-

-le   C'est un léger papillon,   Le petit coeur Ninon."

("Ninon's tiny heart is so little, so gentle, so fragile. It is a light
butterfly, Ninon's tiny heart.")

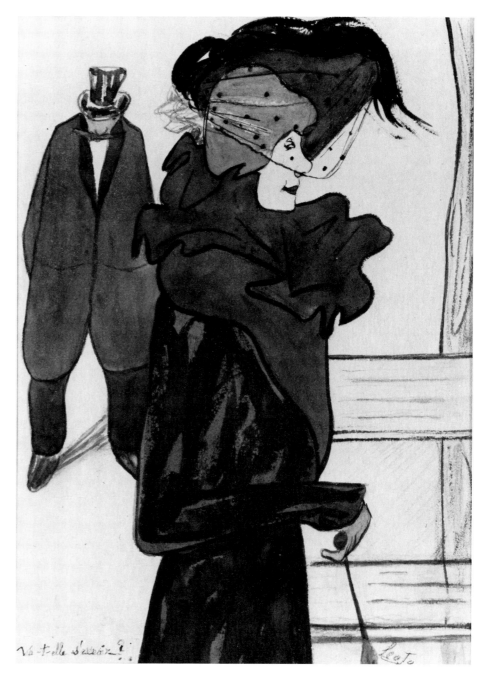

57. "VA-T-ELLE S'ASSEOIR?" ("WILL SHE SIT DOWN?").
    Undated

Gouache and pencil on drawing paper, text in ink.

26.0 x 18.0 cm.

Leo Jo; Va-t-elle s'asseoir?
Coll. W.D. No. 5715.

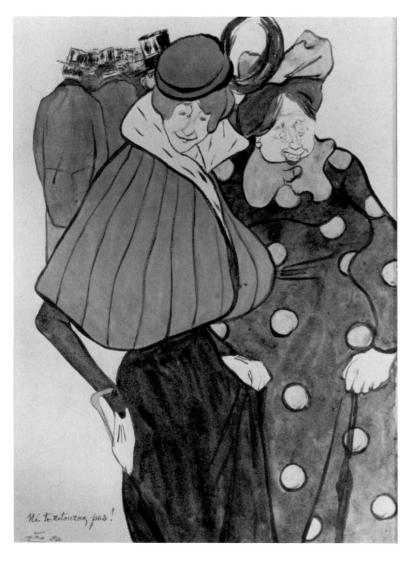

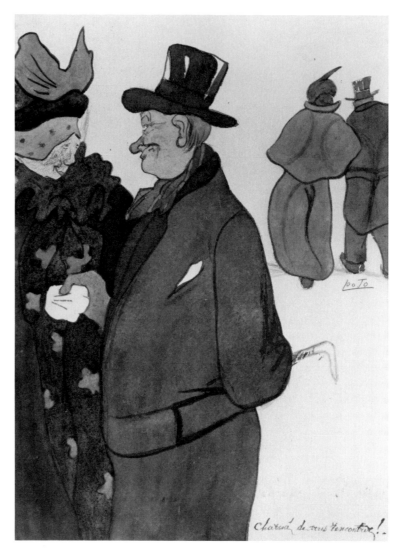

58. "NE TE RETOURNE PAS!" ("DON'T TURN AROUND!").
  Undated

Gouache on drawing paper, text in ink.

25.5 x 17.8 cm.

Leo Jo; Ne te retourne pas!
Coll. W.D. No. 5756.

59. "CHARMÉ DE VOUS RENCONTRER!" ("PLEASED TO MEET YOU!").
  Undated

Gouache and pencil on drawing paper.

25.0 x 18.0 cm.

Leo Jo; Charmé de vous rencontrer!
Coll. W.D. No. 5749.

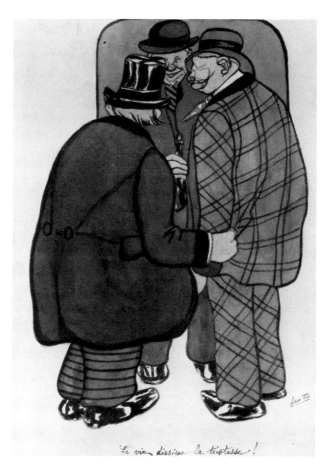

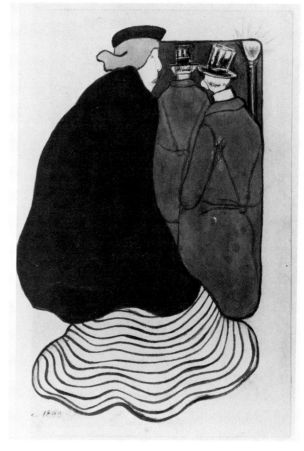

60. "C'TE TROTTE EN VILLE!" ("ON THE GO IN TOWN!").
  Undated

Gouache on drawing paper, text in ink.

25.5 x 17.8 cm.

Leo Jo; C'te trotte en ville!
Coll. W.D. No. 5708.

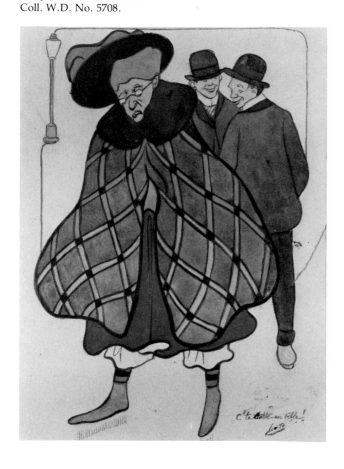

61. "LE VIN DISSIPE LA TRISTESSE!" ("WINE DISPELS
  SADNESS!"). Undated

Gouache on drawing paper, text in ink.

26.0 x 18.0 cm.

Leo Jo; Le vin dissipe la tristesse!
Coll. W.D. No. 5726.

62. "SILHOUETTE 1900." Undated

Gouache on drawing paper, text in pencil.

26.2 x 18.0 cm.

Leo Jo; Silhouette 1900, des . . . (old text obliterated).
Coll. W.D. No. 5709.

63. FIGURES IN EVENING DRESS. 1898

Gray gouache on drawing paper.

26.2 x 17.0 cm.; the left side of the paper has been cropped,
and part of the cloak has been cut around.

Unsigned; dated 1898 (remainder of text has been cut out).
Coll. W.D. No. 5724.

64. "LES BELLES PLUMES AUX BEAUX OISEAUX!"
  ("THE GRANDE DAME IN HER FINE FEATHERS!")
  Undated

Gouache and pencil on drawing paper.

36.0 x 27.5 cm.

Léo Jo; Les belles plumes aux beaux oiseaux!
Coll. W.D. No. 5772.

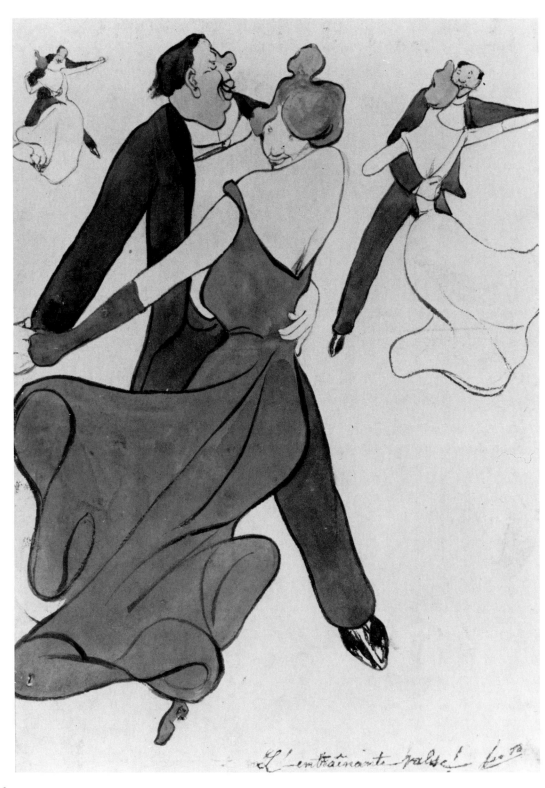

65. "L'ENTRAÎNANTE VALSE!" ("THE CATCHY WALTZ!"). Undated
Gouache on drawing paper, text in ink.
24.5 × 18.0 cm.
Leo Jo; L'entraînante valse!
Coll. W.D. No. 5768.

One can almost hear the figures in the foreground murmuring as they circle the floor to the strains of "Fascination":

> *Je t'ai rencontré simplement,*
> *Et tu n'as rien fait pour chercher à me plaire,*
> *Je t'aime pourtant*
> *D'un amour ardent . . .*

(from "Fascination";
music by F.D. Marchetti, lyrics by Maurice de Féraudy)

while those at left hum the "Heure Exquise" waltz, written to the tune of Franz Lehar's "The Merry Widow";

> *Heure exquise qui nous grise lentement!*

(adaptation in French (1909) by Gaston de Caillavet and Robert de Flers)

and at right, the "Reviens!" waltz (1910):

> *Reviens! veux-tu?*
> *Ton absence a brisé ma vie,*
> *Aucune femme, vois-tu,*
> *N'a jamais pris ta place en mon coeur, amie . . .*

(words and music by Fragson and Christine)

66. "DE L'ALLURE!" ("LOOKING GRAND!"). Undated
Gouache on drawing paper, text in ink and pencil.
25.5 x 17.8 cm.
Leo Jo; De l'allure! . . . written in ink as well as in pencil at bottom of skirt.
Coll. W.D. No. 5747.

This design appears in a photograph of Léo Jo in her studio.

(See also Léo Jo: *Child with Cookie*, No. 43.)

Alfred Ruhemann, *Jung Belgien*, Berlin, n.d., p. 15.

67. WARMLY DRESSED WOMAN. Undated
Gouache on drawing paper.
23.0 x 16.0 cm.
Léo Jo.
Coll. W.D. No. 5714.

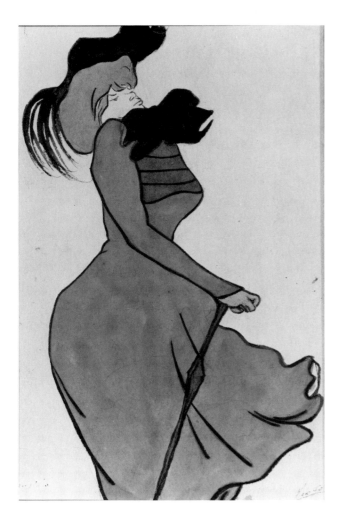

beggar, buy a bouquet of violets from a vendor, with the same curiosity with which I would have watched a great painter wield his brush. And when, reaching my side, she greeted me with a slight smile, it was as if she had made for me a delicate wash drawing, a masterpiece, and added to it a dedication."

Marcel Proust, "À la recherche du temps perdu," *La Pléiade*, Paris, p. 144.

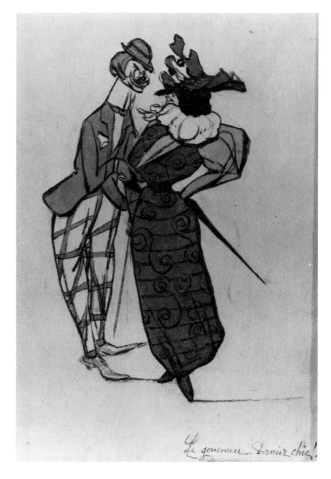

68. "COQ ANGLAIS." Undated

Gouache on drawing paper, text in ink.

25.5 x 17.5 cm.

Leo Jo; Coq anglais.
Coll. W.D. No. 5748.

Doesn't this young woman evoke Proust's description of the Duchess of Guermantes: "I told myself that the woman I saw walking in the distance, opening her parasol, crossing the street, was, in the opinion of connoisseurs, the greatest living master of the art of perfecting gestures and making something charming out of them. Yet she moved forward unaware of this reputation. Her small **rebellious** body, unaware of its effect, was obliquely arched beneath a violet surah scarf; her clear, sulky eyes looked listlessly in front of her and had perhaps noticed me. She bit the corner of her lip; I watched her lift her muff, give alms to a

69. "LE GOMMEUX DERNIER CHIC!" ("THE FASHION PLATE!"). Undated

Gouache on drawing paper.

23.8 x 15.5 cm.

Unsigned; Le gommeu [sic] Dernier chic!
Coll. W.D. No. 5750.

The "café-concert" soon saw its performers categorized by distinct types: the *pierreuses*, the *comiques-grimes*, in the melodramatic repertory: *La Tasse de lait, Roule train du plaisir, l'Hirondelle du faubourg, L'Entrecôte,* and *L'Étoile du marin,* who were often dressed in black, a "small red scarf knotted around the neck, with a triangle of fabric lying on the shoulder" in the style begun by Angèle Moreau. "*La gommeuse* (the 'fashion plate') joined the popular terminology when Henriette Bepoix had the idea of wearing a hooded cape, carrying a parasol, and giving herself airs. The masculine counterpart, *le gommeux* (the 'swell'), was best represented by Libert, who charmed sensitive souls by singing *L'Amant d'Amanda.*" Among other types of performers there were also: the *tourlourou,* the *comique excentrique,* the *vieux beau,* the *chanteur agité,* and the *patriotique.*

Georges Coulonges, *La chanson en son temps: De Béranger au juke-box,* Paris, 1969, pp. 32, 33.

PRIVAT ANTIONE THÉODORE LIVEMONT
(Schaerbeek, 1861–Schaerbeek, 1936)

Decorator, poster designer, illustrator, professor

Upon completion of his studies at l'École des Arts Décoratifs in Saint-Josse-ten-Noode—where some years later he would be a professor alongside Adolphe Crespin—Livemont received a scholarship that allowed him to visit Paris. There he was engaged by Lamaire to decorate a portion of the City Hall, but a new law soon prohibited foreigners from working on official projects. He then found work at Lavastres, and in 1885 he helped create the stage designs for "Hamlet" at the Théâtre Français. He also helped Duvignaud survey the valuable furniture belonging to the Comédie Française. At night he took courses at l'École Etienne-Marcel under Delaporte. In 1889, after six years of work in Paris, he established himself at Schaerbeek, where he received many commissions, including the decoration of the Provincial Government building at Hasselt, the dome of the Mors' mansion in Passy (Paris), and the Rey lingerie and linen store in Brussels.

In 1890 he drew his first poster for an exposition at Schaerbeek. In 1891 he created a poster for an exposition at Saint-Josse-ten-Noode; and in 1893, 1895, 1896 and later he designed posters for Le Cercle Artistique de Schaerbeek (see No. 88). Soon he was a confirmed poster artist and by 1900 he had produced about thirty posters. His interest in lithography led him to become a printer as well.

He was a virtuoso poster lithographer, always drawing the image on the stone himself. Woman was almost his sole subject, and he created a type to which he remained faithful: with heavy eyelids and straight lashes, heart-shaped mouth, long tresses strewn with soft flowers or restrained by a startling hair ornament, rich gowns with diaphanous sleeves, slender fingers—nails filed to a point—displaying a product for sale. The delicate aspect of woman was emphasized by a fine, complex coloration, often set against an aura of light and framed with a rich design.

From 1900 on, Octave Maus recognized that "it was easy to discover certain analogies between the posters of Privat Livemont and those of Mucha . . . Perhaps the inquiry, far from hurting M. Privat Livemont, would be in favor of the Brussels artist whose first posters go back to 1890, that is to say, to a period when the name of Mucha was unknown." (Maus, p. 59).

The Secret Livemont

"Je fais souvent ce rêve étrange et pénétrant
D'une femme inconnue et que j'aime et qui m'aime
Et qui n'est, chaque fois, ni tout à fait la même
Ni tout à fait une autre, et m'aime et me comprends."

(Verlaine, "Mon rêve familier" in *Les Poèmes Saturniens*, VI, 1867, republished in 1890)

This mysterious woman, who haunts Verlaine's dreams as "neither exactly the same person nor exactly another person," and who loves and understands him, may also be found throughout Livemont's work; she imparts a dreamlike quality to each subject he treats. Outwardly she appears a soft and gracious creature. In reality, if one observes her pose, her finery, and the setting in which she performs, everything changes subtly. To the charm of the advertisement and the quality of the graphic ability is added a third force, literary and symbolic. The complexity of the imagery varies from one work to another. Sometimes it is only a matter of a happy match in the choice of a flower and the subject treated; sometimes there are many evocative signs, attesting to Livemont's thorough knowledge of both modern literature and the classics.

The following ideas result from a close study of the posters and a knowledge of the era.

Simple imagery: In *Cacao Van Houten* (No. 93) we see the crysanthemum, an autumn flower: how good it feels to have a cup of hot chocolate when it is cold and rainy! For children, Livemont chooses the delicate and tender flowers of Spring: wild roses, peach blossoms, periwinkles. An attentive mother watches over their joyous frolics; should the need arise, she knows how to soothe and heal using one or another plant with medicinal qualities, such as the chamomile and dandelion (No. 102), or elderberries (No. 97). The chestnut tree (Nos. 92, 97, 103) serves as a focal point for numerous family and artistic activities: Planted by order of King Léopold II in the center of the wide avenues that link the forest to the city of Brussels, this tree is majestic and decorative; its fruit and bark are said to have medicinal value, and it also signals the changes of season.

Complex imagery: In *Bitter Oriental* (No. 90) we see several Oriental themes presented in one provocative composition. The key (or "clef") within the crescent moon invites us to search for meanings; the extended arc, the dark-haired woman, and the crescent moon form an exotic setting. The key to making Oriental bitters is perhaps in the artful mixing of the oil and juices of the orange (in the right hand), and other plants steeped in gin. The oyster shell held in the woman's left hand recalls Bizet's opera, "Les Pêcheurs de Perles" (1863); and the crescent moon brings to mind Victor Hugo's tragic "Clair de Lune" in *Les Orientales* (1829). The serpent bracelet imparts yet more power to the feminine figure.

The poster *Manufacture Royale de Corsets P.D.* (No. 91) is designed around the theme of 'purity' in its broadest sense, embracing uprightness, nobility, inward and outward elegance. Witness the repeated use of the lily, symbol of purity; and the unicorn (in the registered trademark), whose one horn symbolizes a spiritual arrow, a beam of light, the sword of God, and the divine astuteness that is in man. It is one of the favorite symbols of love: think of the marvelous French tapestries of

"The Lady and the Unicorn" in the Cluny Museum.

Bec Auer (No. 86) reflects a religious syncretism that was characteristic of the period. A young woman in a priestly stance wears on her head a crown of lights, with seven branches and a frontal disc; the disc may signify the Egyptian sun or the third Buddhist eye (which represents light from within, from the super-conscience). In her hands she holds what Charles Van Lerberghe would describe as "flowers of light" (*Entrevisions*, 1898).

"The Secret Livemont" is directly inspired by a fascinating report on the literary aspects of Livemont's and Combaz's work, written by Miss Jacqueline Gesquière, professor of literature and philosophy.

Biographical information on Livemont is from: Unedited archives, Coll. W.D.; A.E.I., pp. 105, 114, 115, 130-132; E. De Linge, "Privat Livemont, décorateur et affichiste belge," in *The P.*, London, August/September 1898, no. 3, vol. 1, pp. 98-100; A.B., pp. 49-51 and XIII; Xavier Havermans, "L'Affiche Illustrée: Privat Livemont," in *La Revue Graphique belge*, Brussels, no. 8-9, December 1898-1899, pp. 84-86; O. Maus, "Privat Livemont," in A & D, Paris, Jan.-June 1900, vol. 7, pp. 55-61.

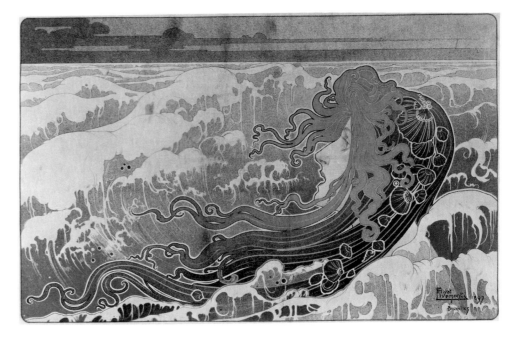

70. LA VAGUE. 1897

Lithograph in pale green, black, gray-green and red, highlighted in gold.

32.0 × 50.0 cm. (motif); complete print c. 48.6 × 69.0 cm.

Privat Livemont, 1897, Bruxelles.
Coll. W.D. No. 886.

"The feverish activity of M. Privat Livemont is not satisfied with the many occasions which require the help of his soft lithographic pencil: he creates other occasions. Here he is hard at work at a new task: to form a print collection of which he himself is editor and in which, in a series of twelve to fifteen plates he may show the results of his many conscientious pursuits.

"*La Vague* is the first of these prints. Printed in four shades . . . and highlighted in gold, it achieves, as an art form, the highest degree of skill. The superimposing of hues, thanks to the perfect registering, varies the effects harmoniously, and the skillful graduation of the tinting gives the entire work an infinite delicacy. If the plates which are currently being executed—and which borrow from various compositions of the artist, some mystical, others purely ornamental—are, as is likely, produced with the same care, the complete set will constitute the most perfect document that color lithography could bequeath to the next century."

(See also Livemont: *Woman Sculpting*, No. 71; *Woman Painting*, No. 72.)

Octave Maus, "Privat Livemont," in A & D, Jan./June 1900, vol. 7, pp. 55, 61.

(Illustrated on page 14)

71. WOMAN SCULPTING. 1901

Lithograph in flesh, rose, bordeaux red, black, greenish-blue, bottle green, light gray.

50.0 × 31.9 cm. (motif); 69.0 × 48.0 cm. the complete print.

Privat Livemont 1901 Brux.; the publisher is probably the artist himself.
Coll. W.D. No. 520.

(See also *La Vague*, No. 70.)

72. WOMAN PAINTING. 1901

Lithograph in flesh, light bistre, black, light gray, bordeaux red, light blue, greenish-blue.

50.2 × 32.1 cm. (motif); 67.5 × 48.6 cm. the complete print.

Privat Livemont 1901 Brux.; the publisher is probably the artist himself.
Coll. W.D. No. 521.

(See also *La Vague*, No. 70.)

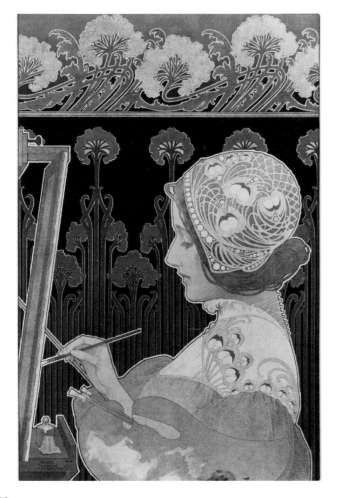

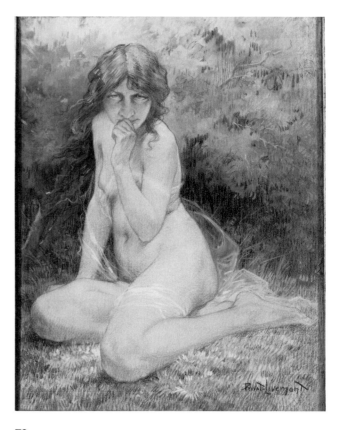

73. NUDE SEATED ON THE GRASS. Undated
Pastel on Ingres paper, mounted on canvas.
55.2 × 42.0 cm.
Privat Livemont.
Coll. W.D. No. 5191.

74. SEATED NUDE. Undated
Black pencil and red chalk on Ingres paper.
46.0 × 29.4 cm.
Unsigned.
Coll. W.D. No. 5201.

75. LEANING FIGURE. Undated
Blue pencil on Ingres paper.
46.0 × 29.5 cm.
Unsigned.
Coll. W.D. 5202.

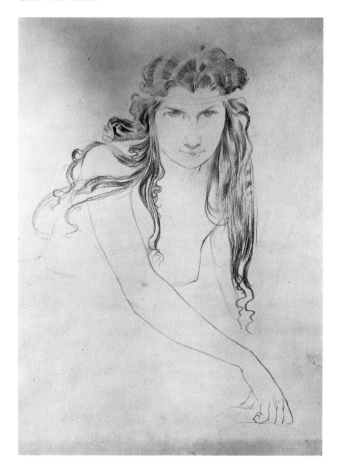

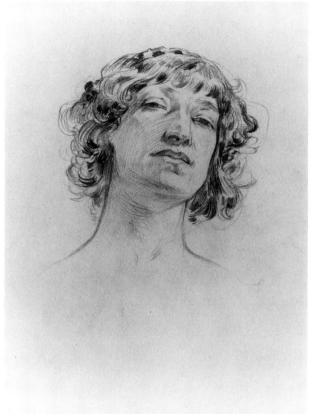

76. HEAD OF A WOMAN. Undated
Black pencil on drawing paper.
46.4 × 30.4 cm.
Unsigned.
Coll. W.D. No. 5203.

77. THREE DANCERS. Undated
Pastel on blue paper.
30.0 × 21.8 cm.
Unsigned.
Coll. W.D. No. 5171.

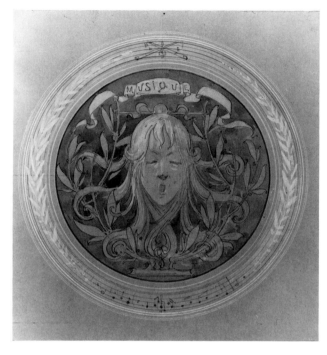

78. DESIGN FOR A MEDALLION: "MUSIQUE." Undated
Watercolor and pencil on light gray pasteboard.
15.6 × 16.0 cm.; diameter of image 13.5 cm.
Unsigned; musique.
Coll. W.D. No. 5170.

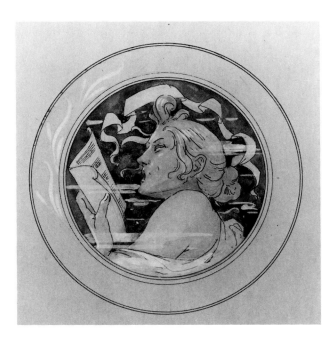

79. DESIGN FOR A MEDALLION: SONGSTRESS. Undated

Watercolor and black ink on light gray pasteboard.

15.6 × 16.3 cm.; diameter of image 13.5 cm.

Unsigned.
Coll. W.D. No. 5169.

81. DESIGN FOR A FESTIVAL PROGRAM: "VENETIA."
Undated

Pen drawing on paper highlighted with pale pink and orange wash.

27.4 × 39.6 cm.

Privat Livemont (in pencil, lower left, barely legible); Bruxelles, Venise, Venetia, Programme Officiel des Fêtes. The pasteboard on which the design is glued bears the seal of the artist: Privat Livemont, Peintre-Décorateur-Dessinateur, 95 rue Renkin 95, Schaerbeek-Bruxelles.
Coll. W.D. 5184.

80. DESIGN FOR A MEDALLION: MUSE. Undated

Pencil drawing and wash on paper.

Diameter 30.5 cm.; outer dimensions 60.0 × 46.2 cm.
Coll. W.D. No. 5176.

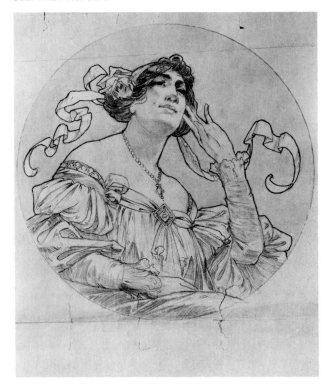

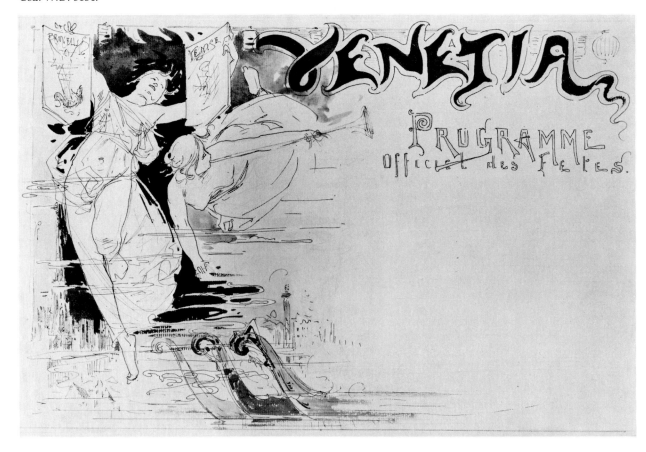

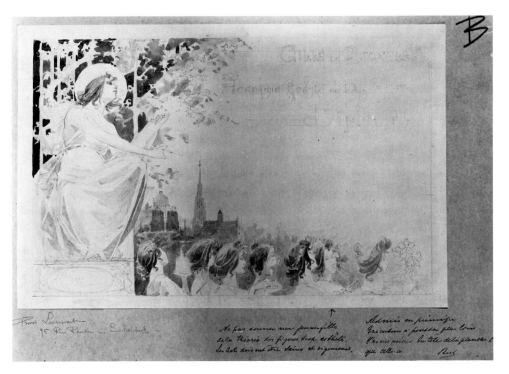

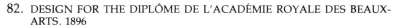

82. DESIGN FOR THE DIPLÔME DE L'ACADÉMIE ROYALE DES BEAUX-
    ARTS. 1896

Pencil and wash (cameo gray on pale bistre background) on paper.

27.5 × 41.3 cm.

Ville de Bruxelles, Académie Royale des Beaux-Arts, Diplôme, sceau. The
pasteboard on which the artist has mounted the design bears his signature in
pencil: Privat Livemont, 95 rue Renkin—Schaerbeek. There is also a large "B" in
blue pencil, and a note written in ink by the mayor, Charles Buls (if the signature
has been correctly identified): "Ne pas donner aux jeunes filles de la théorie des
figures trop esthètes. Les Arts doivent être sains et vigoureux. Admis en
principe. Exécution à pousser plus loin. J'aime mieux la tête de la planche A que
celle-ci. BULS."
Coll. W.D. No. 5180.

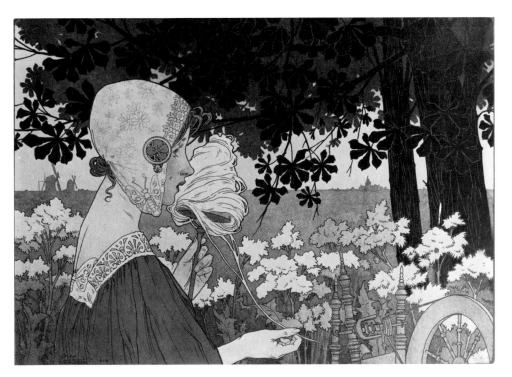

83. WOMAN SPINNING. 1904

Lithograph in yellow, flesh, red, blue, olive green and dark gray.

There is a zinc transfer where *Woman Spinning* and *Woman Embroidering* are
reproduced side by side.

27.4 × 37.4 cm. (motif)

Privat Livemont 1904; the publisher is probably the artist himself.
Coll. W.D. No. 5213.

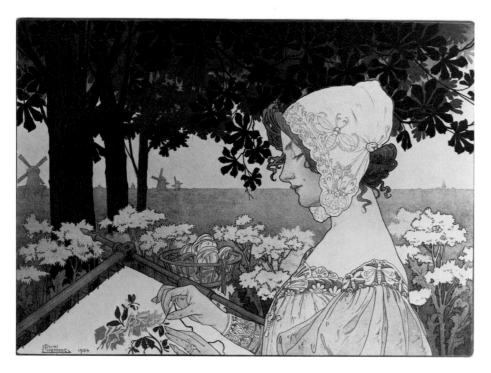

84. WOMAN EMBROIDERING. 1904

Lithograph in yellow, flesh, red, blue, olive green and dark gray.

27.4 × 37.2 cm. (motif)

Privat Livemont, 1904; the publisher is probably the artist himself.
Coll. W.D. No. 5212.

85. ABSINTHE ROBETTE. 1896

Lithograph in yellow, flesh, reddish-brown, light blue and dark green (draw-ing).

110.0 × 82.4 cm.

Privat Livemont, 1896; des presses de J.L. Goffart, lithographe, Bruxelles. Their seal on the fiscal stamps is dated 7 October 1896.
Coll. W.D. No. 266.
St. P. 1897 cat. no. 157.

This poster was a great success, and 500 copies were printed. Ten years later a Belgian law (of 25 September 1906) forbade the importation, production, sale, purchase or transportation of absinthe because of its poisonous properties when taken to excess.

The 7th International Congress to combat alcoholism was held in Brussels in the autumn of 1897; it brought together politicians, scholars and doctors from many countries including the U.S.A., Australia and Russia.

Communication from Mr. Deboe, director of the Comité National pour l'étude et la préservation de l'alcoolisme, 94 chaussée de Vleurgat, Brussels.

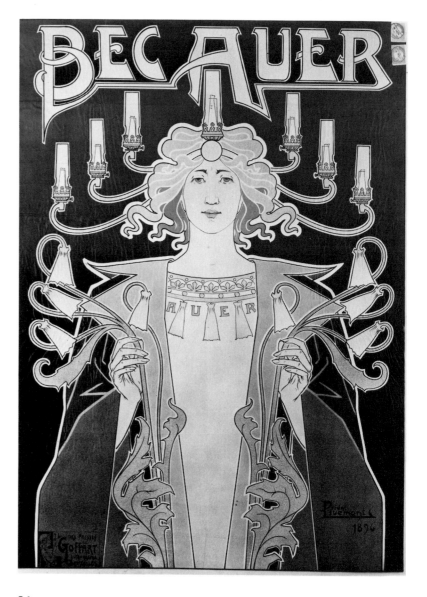

86. BEC AUER. 1896

Lithograph in yellow, rose, medium blue, dark blue (drawing—grained stone), gray (on the bottom of the poster), becoming sky blue (the eyes) because of a divided ink-fountain.

111.5 × 80.0 cm.

Privat Livemont 1896; des presses de J.L. Goffart, lithographe, Bruxelles.
Coll. W.D. No. 164.
St. P. 1897 cat. no. 155.

The Bec Auer Von Welsbach consists of an ordinary Bunsen burner covered with a fabric hood (cotton or wool) specially treated with zirconium, lanthanum or yttrium oxides. When the burner was lit, a considerable amount of heat would build up inside the hood, causing it to glow with a very bright light.

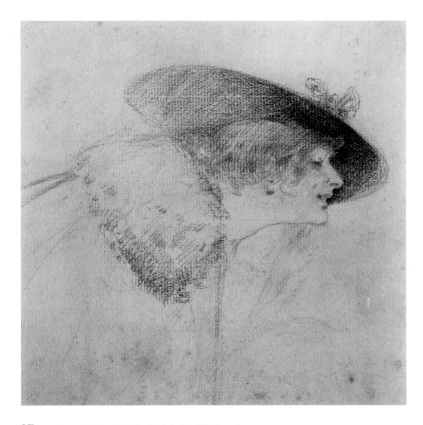

87. WOMAN IN A FUR COLLAR. Undated

Black and red chalk on Ingres paper.

29.5 × 28.0 cm. approximately.

Unsigned.
Coll. W.D. No. 5190.

This is probably a preparatory drawing for the poster *Cercle artistique de Rouge Cloitre*, 1917 (Coll. W.D. No. 5215).

88. CERCLE ARTISTIQUE DE SCHAERBEEK (AT THE STATUETTE). 1897

Lithograph in orange, red, bistre-black (grained stone), dark green background (mechanically graded tint), bistre-green (slightly mechanically graded tint) and gold.

105.5 × 78.0 cm.

Privat Livemont 1897, Bruxelles; Trommer & Staeves, 65, rue Vanderlinden, Bruxelles. The text, at top, reads: Cercle Artistique de Schaerbeek, 5e Exposition Annuelle, Ouverte du 6 au 30 mai, 253, rue Royale (Galerie Manteau), Entrée: 50 Centimes, le jour de l'Ouverture: 5 Fr.
Coll. W.D. No. 169bis.
The P. Oct. 1898, p. 165; St. P. 1897 cat. no. 160.

The donkeys and cherries in the border design are the time-honored, unofficial emblems of the Schaerbeek commune. At dawn the farmers of this prosperous region would drive their donkeys through the Schaerbeek Gate (formerly the Cologne Gate), the passage point to the Brussels market. The local people, awakened by the donkeys' braying, came to associate the donkey with a person from Schaerbeek. From the 18th century on, Schaerbeek has been known for the quality of its cherries; one variety is used to make *kriek*, a special Brussels beer that is drunk with a bit of sugar.

R. Van Den Haute, "Messire Aliboron de Schaerbeek," in *Les Cahiers de l'ancien Saint-Josse*, Brussels, 1967, no. 4, pp. 55-66.

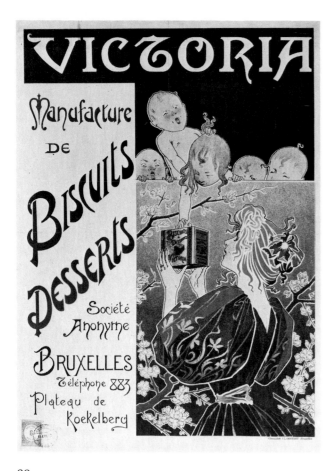

89. VICTORIA. 1897

Lithograph in yellow, rose, red, black, light blue, gray.

54.0 × 38.5 cm.

A.T.P.L. 97; chromolith J. L. Goffart, Bruxelles. Their seal appended to the fiscal stamps is dated 13 April 1897.
Coll. W.D. No. 257.

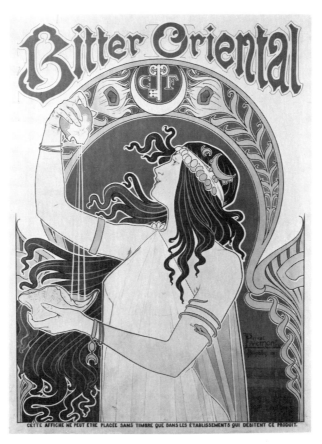

90. BITTER ORIENTAL. 1897

Lithograph in ochre, flesh (machine shaded), red, blue and black (drawing).

110.5 × 83.1 cm.

Privat Livemont 1897; des presses de J. L. Goffart, lithographe, Bruxelles. Their seal appended to the fiscal stamps is dated 5 April 1897.
Coll. W.D. No. 167.
St. P. 1897 cat. no. 156.

This is an advertisement for a liquor made by steeping various herbs in gin.

91. MANUFACTURE ROYALE DE CORSETS P.D. 1897

Lithograph on grained stone in yellow, flesh, pink, red-brown, light blue, dark blue, gray, violet and black (drawing).

72.9 × 47.7 cm.

Privat Livemont 1897, Bruxelles; no printer's name.
Coll. W.D. No. 172.

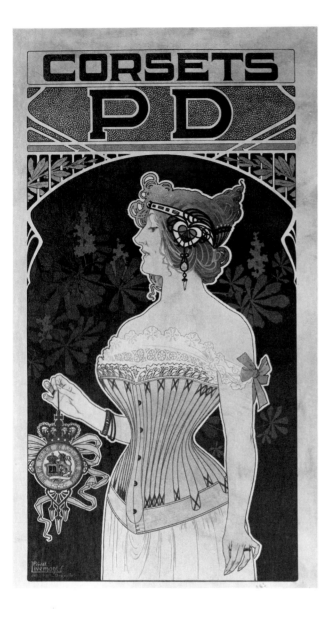

92. CORSETS P.D. Undated

Lithograph on grained stone in flesh, warm (light) bistre, pale green, dark blue-green, dark brown, red and gold.

53.6 × 29.6 cm.

Privat Livemont; del Edit. Bruxelles.
Coll. W.D. No. 887.

The corset reappeared around 1830. Who would save our grandmothers from them? The models began to lose their rigidity with the appearance of the stretchable corset (1903) and the elastic belt (1904). Poiret, the famous French couturier, banished all such constraining items in 1908. Under their flowing gowns women began wearing corset-girdles made of stretchable knitted silk, without steel or whalebone stays.

Bibliothèque des Arts Décoratifs, Paris, vol. 222/1: clothing and various objects, 222/2: corsets from A to Z; M. Delpierre, *Modes de la Belle Époque. Costumes français 1890-1910 et portraits, exposition*, catalogue of exhibition at the Musée du Costume, Paris, November 1961-March 1962; Dr. Gaches-Sarraute, *Le corset, Étude physiologique et pratique*, Paris, 1900; M. Leloir, *Dictionnaire du costume et de ses accessoires, des armes et des étoffes, des origines à nos jours*, Paris, 1961.

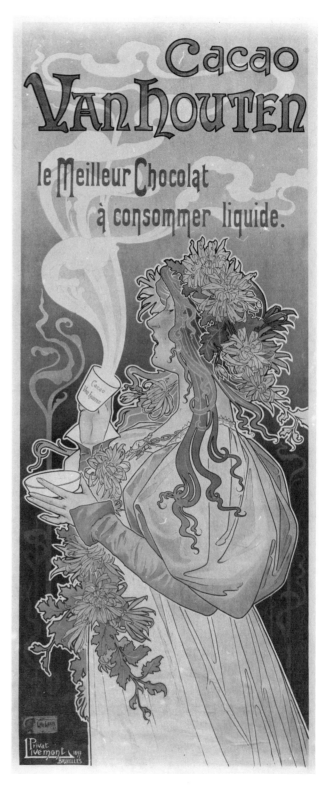

93. CACAO VAN HOUTEN. 1897

Lithograph in yellow, buff, flesh, light blue, dark blue, pink, dark gray (drawing), red and blue (text). The slogan was inserted, as it was varied according to the country where the product was sold.

151.5 × 62.7 cm.

Privat Livemont 1897, Bruxelles; chromolithographie L. Van Leer & Cie, Amsterdam.
Coll. W.D. No. 171.

Cocoa is native to Mexico. It first appeared in Europe in the 16th century via the Iberian Peninsula, and by the beginning of the 18th century it was enjoyed with relative frequency.

A.M. Marien-Dugardin, *La vie au XVIIIe siècle*, exhibition at the Musées royaux d'art et d'histoire, Brussels, 1970, pp. 73-77.

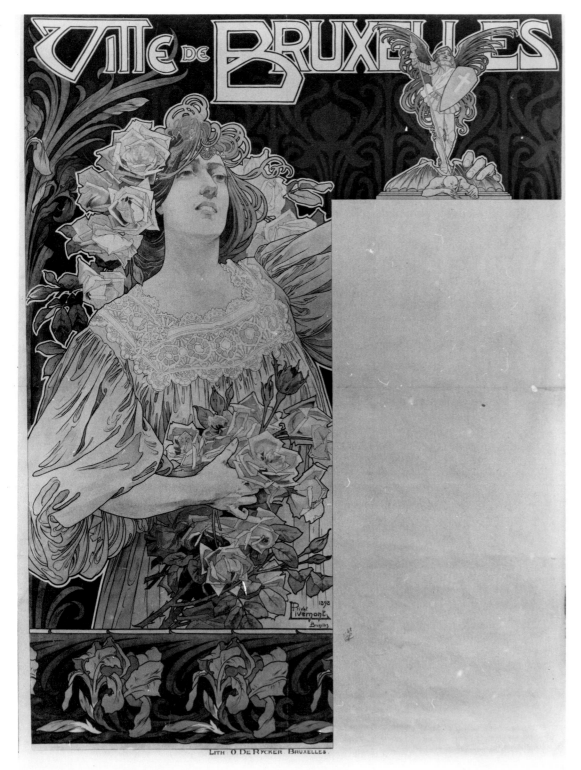

LITH. O. DE RYCKER BRUXELLES.

94. VILLE DE BRUXELLES. 1898

Lithograph in yellow, pink, scarlet, lacquer red (i.e. blueish-red), chocolate brown (drawing), light blue, medium blue becoming dark blue in the interior border by split-fountain inking, mauve and gray.

153.0 × 110.5 cm.

Privat Livemont 1898, Bruxelles. Written in ink, the number 48 and the artist's initials; lith. O. De Rycker, Bruxelles.
Coll. W.D. No. 173.

Ten thousand copies of this poster were printed. It was used each summer for Independence Day on July 21, and the text was modified accordingly. In her hand the young woman holds a statuette of the patron of the city of Brussels: St. Michael slaying the dragon. The iris is the flower of Brussels. At one time thousands of irises carpeted the marshland and vast areas where the city now stands, making a beautiful countryside.

The woman's gracious smile causes one to recall a significant fact: In 1974 Belgium, and especially Brussels, housed more than 500 of the world's 4,000-plus international associations, putting Brussels after Paris but before London, Geneva and New York as a major center of international activity—a position the city has held since 1910, when it was the site of the First World Congress of International Associations. Of similar interest, in 1909 Auguste Beernaert, founder and president of the Union of International Associations, was awarded the Nobel Peace Prize—one of three Belgians to receive the prize between 1904-1913. Still another indication of this international interest was a Belgian law of 1919 (modified in 1954) granting civil status to any international association which had philanthropic, religious, scientific, artistic or pedagogical goals, and which counted among its administrators at least one Belgian national (most countries required a majority of nationals).

(See also Combaz: *Premier Congrès International des Avocats*, No. 1.)

O. Maus, "Privat Livemont," in A&D, Paris, 1900 vol. 7, p. 61; Georges-Patrick Speeckaert, "Belgique, terre de coopération internationale. 1: De la liberté à la solidarité," in *Le Soir*, Brussels, 14 December 1974, p. 5, and Robert Fenaux, *idem.*, "2. Bruxelles, centre mondial d'association," *op. cit.*, 17 December 1974.

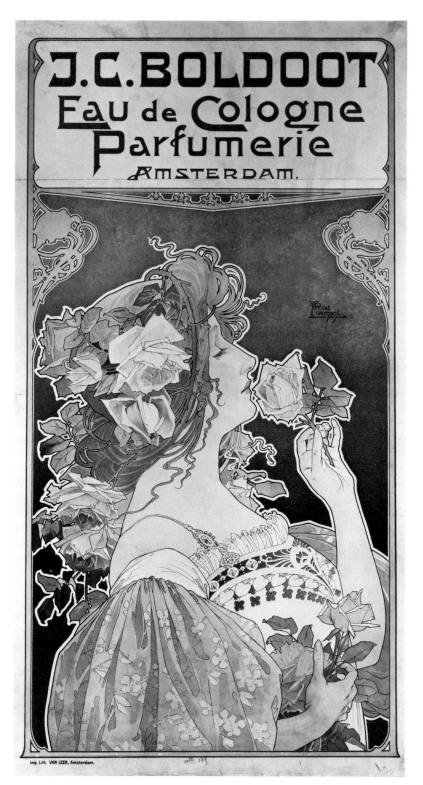

95. J. C. BOLDOOT. Undated

Lithograph on grained stone in yellow, flesh, pink, light blue, dark gray (drawing) and red.

74.8 × 40.2 cm.

Privat Livemont; imp. lith. Van Leer, Amsterdam.
Coll. W.D. No. 179.
E & A, August 1899, p. 180.

(Illustrated on page 14)

96. HELM CACAO. 1899

Lithograph in yellow, dark brown, flesh, pink, red, light blue, blue, and light bistre.

153.0 × 66.0 cm.

Privat Livemont. The poster was printed by Van Leer in Amsterdam and had the following text: Nederlandsche Cacaofabriek. Helmond Holland. The design for the poster, Coll. W.D. No. 1525, is dated 1899.
Coll. W. D. No. 889.
The P., December 1900, vol. 5, no. 29, p. 144.

(See also Livemont: *Cacao Van Houten,* No. 93.)

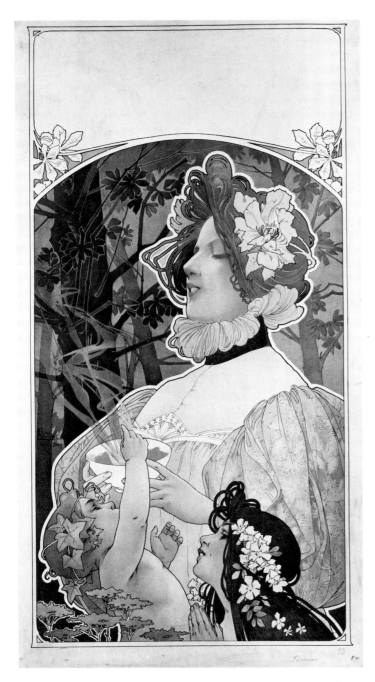

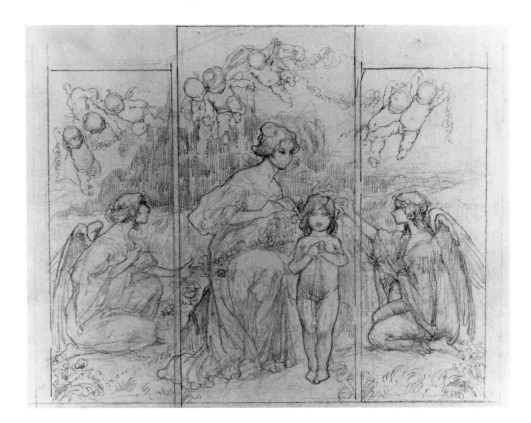

98. PREPARATORY SKETCH FOR A POSTER: PALAIS DE
LA FEMME. 1900

Pencil drawing on paper; the paper bears the watermark:
Nevada Vellum E.H. & C.

21.6 × 27.6 cm.

Unsigned.
Coll. W.D. No. 5153.

97. CACAO A. DRIESSEN (ROTTERDAM). 1900

Lithograph in yellow, pink, deep pink, light blue, gray, dark
brown, and red (title).

77.0 × 40.5 cm.

Privat Livemont 1900 Brux.; Van Leer, Amsterdam.
Coll. W.D. No. 175.

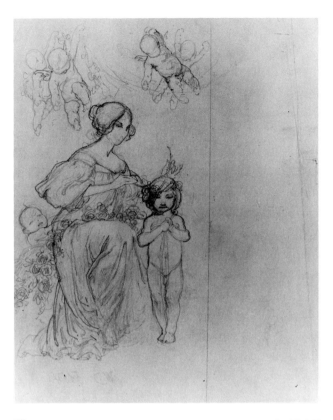

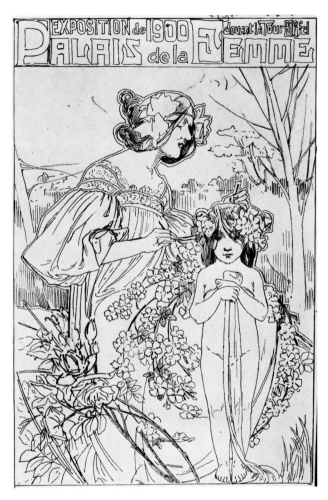

99. PREPARATORY SKETCH FOR A POSTER: PALAIS DE
LA FEMME. 1900

Pencil drawing on paper; the paper bears the watermark:
Nevada Vellum E.H. & C.

21.6 × 27.6 cm. (paper); 21.6 × 13.8 (motif).

Unsigned.
Coll. W.D. No. 5154.

100. POSTER DESIGN: PALAIS DE LA FEMME. 1900

Print after an original drawing.

20.3 × 13.2 cm.

Unsigned.
Coll. W.D. No. 1809.

The poster appears in The P., December 1900, p. 143.

101. TROPON CHOCOLADE (MÜLHEIM-RHEIN). 1900

Lithograph in yellow, flesh, deep pink, red, light blue, dark
blue and bistre.

61.0 × 35.8 cm.

Privat Livemont 1900 Brux.; Chromolith. O. De Rycker & Mendel, Bruxelles. The poster is initialled by Livemont (P.L.) and
numbered (no. 20) in ink at lower right.
Coll. W.D. No. 176.
The P., December 1900, p. 144; published without the text.

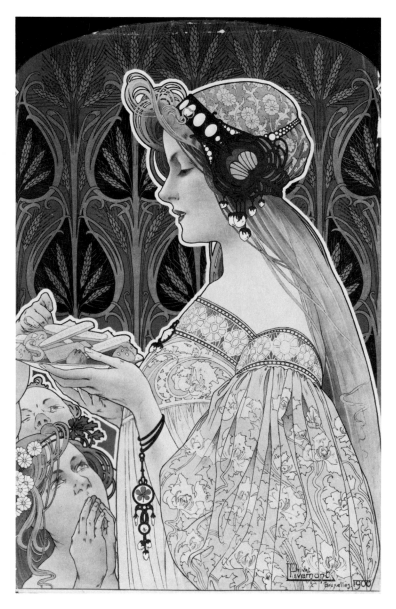

102. BISCUITS DE BEUKELAER. 1900
Lithograph in yellow, flesh, pink, red, light blue, dark blue, soft black and gold.

80.3 x 44.6 cm.

Privat Livemont Bruxelles. 1900.
Coll. W.D. No. 177.

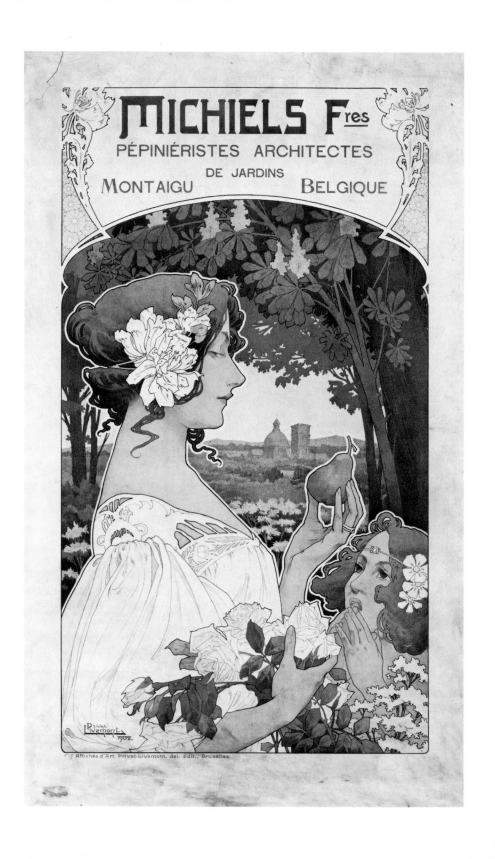

103. MICHIELS FRES. PÉPINIÉRISTES. 1902

Lithograph in yellow, flesh, bistre, green and brown.

86.0 × 50.5 cm.

Privat Livemont 1902; Affiches d'Art. Privat Livemont, del. Edit., Bruxelles.
Coll. W.D. No. 519.

"If the 16th century is the golden age of Belgian history, the 19th century could be called the age of flowers. Belgium begins to resemble a huge garden" (Balis, p. 51). Jan Balis, in his catalogue *Hortus Belgicus*, recounts the often surprising ways in which political and historical events influenced the plant trade. For example, the Empress Joséphine succeeded in circumventing the Continental blockade in the interest of her gardens at Malmaison, probably the most beautiful in Europe, by calling upon an official "botanical chargé d'affaires" as well as upon the Belgian blockade runners.

"Of course, not all plants imported secretly go to Paris; some remain in Belgium. . .and one could say that they mark the beginning of a trade from which Belgium will gain worldwide attention" (ibid., p. 53). A significant political event was the signing, at Ghent, of a peace treaty between the United States and England on 24 December 1814. The Americans were honored with a great exhibition organized by the Société Royale d'Agriculture et de Botanique of Ghent, which dedicated to them a beautiful rose—"The Congress of Ghent"—created by Alexandre Verschaffelt (ibid., p. 55). Charmed and impressed by this welcome, the American delegates henceforth encouraged the importation of large numbers of Belgian plants into the U.S., and American seeds were made available to Belgian horticulturists and collectors.

Fruit and tree cultivation (pomology and dendrology) made as many advances as horticulture. In the poster shown here, the woman holds what is undoubtedly a Comice pear—one of the 818 varieties of pears listed in Adolphe Papeleu's catalogue of 1851. The catalogue also cites 265 varieties of apples, 86 different kinds of peaches, and 205 types of gooseberries (ibid., p. 75). By the spring of 1834, "more than 300 varieties of Flemish pears had been introduced into Boston" (ibid., p. 76).

The exportation of these varieties to the rest of the world became possible when Jean Baptiste van Mons (1765-1842)—pharmacist, doctor, chemist, physicist and horticulturist—developed a procedure whereby shoots from fruit trees could be shipped great distances in order to be grafted.

King Léopold II on many occasions encouraged advances in dendrology. In 1900 he made the nation a gift of 125 hectares of his own private forestland at Tervueren, where Professor Charles Bommer of the Université Libre de Bruxelles established in 1902 an experimental station for introducing foreign trees into Belgium. This station was conceived on both a geographic and dendrological basis (ibid., p. 78).

The firm of Michiels Brothers (Gustave, Édouard, Edmond and Oscar) is still in existence. The founders, who employed more than 100 gardeners, were great specialists in roses and their cultivation, and they edited a compendium of advice and information entitled *La Rose, Reine des Fleurs* (Montaigu, 1912), dedicated to Queen Elisabeth of Belgium.

(See also: Combaz, *Orchids and Butterfly*, No. 37; and *Orchids*, No. 38.)

Jan Balis, *Hortus Belgicus*, Bibliothèque Albert I, Brussels, August-September 1962; information on Michiels Fres given by Mme Julia Michiels, a member of the firm, and by her niece, Mme Robert Bodson.

PHOTO CREDITS:

All photographs are by Louis Loose and the Wittamer-De Camps archives with the exception of Cat. Nos. 1 (W.D. 42), 3 (W.D. 51bis), 4 (W.D. 43), 5 (W.D. 45), 7 (W.D. 50), 9 (W.D. 1509), 12 (W.D. 34), 42 (W.D. 127) and 90 (W.D. 167), which are by Morian.